COUNCIL ON ISLAMIC EDUCATION

Teaching About Islam and Muslims

in the Public School Classroom

3rd Edition

© Copyright 1995 Council on Islamic Education
9300 Gardenia Avenue #B-3
Fountain Valley, California 92708 U.S.A.
tel: 714-839-2929 • fax: 714-839-2714
website: www.cie.org • info@cie.org

Library of Congress Cataloging-in-Publications Data

Council on Islamic Education
Teaching About Islam and Muslims in the Public School Classroom.

ISBN: 1-930109-00-8

1 - Islam - - Study and teaching.
2 - Civilization, Islam - - Study and teaching.
3 - World History - - Study and teaching.
4 - Multicultural Education.

Third Edition, 1415 A.H./October, 1995 C.E.
Seventh Printing, November 2002

Research/Compilation/Typesetting:	Munir A. Shaikh
Cover Design (Dome of the Rock, Jerusalem):	Behzad Tabatabai

To the reader:

Muslims pronounce a blessing upon Prophet Muhammad whenever they mention him by name. The Arabic blessing ﷺ means "may the blessings and peace of Allah be upon him." Although this formula is not printed within the text of this book, it is intended that it be inserted in any reading by a Muslim.

The section on usage of terms in *Part 2 — Teaching with Sensitivity* is excerpted from the Council on Islamic Education's curriculum guide *Strategies and Structures for Presenting World History, with Islam and Muslim History as a Case Study*.

Arabic terms associated with Islam, with the exception of names of people and places, and a few other words, have been set in *italic* type. Most of these terms may be found in the *Quick Reference Glossary*.

Dates are given in terms of the common era (C.E.), a convention referring to the common human experience, devoid of specific religious connotations.

This handbook for educators is listed on the State of California's *Instructional Materials Approved for Legal Compliance* list. Thus, each California school district may use up to 30% of its Instructional Materials Fund (IMF) allocation to purchase this resource.

COUNCIL ON ISLAMIC EDUCATION

The Council on Islamic Education is a national, non-profit resource organization for K-12 textbook publishers, education officials and policymakers, curriculum developers, teachers, and other education professionals. CIE is comprised of scholars of history, religion, education and related disciplines resident at major universities and institutions throughout the United States. These affiliated scholars serve as advisors and participate in various CIE services, activities and events. Educators, writers, concerned parents, students, and volunteers provide additional support for the organization.

Shabbir Mansuri   Founding Director
Saghir A. Aslam   Fund Development Director
Munir A. Shaikh   Publications/Special Projects

Affiliated Scholars

Khalid Y. Blankinship, Assoc. Professor of Religion	Temple University, Philadelphia, PA
Rkia E. Cornell, Research Assoc. Professor of Arabic	University of Arkansas, Fayetteville, AK
Vincent J. Cornell, Director, Middle East Stds. Ctr.	University of Arkansas, Fayetteville, AK
Susan L. Douglass, Principal Researcher & Writer	Council on Islamic Education
Marcia Hermansen, Professor of Religious Studies	Loyola University, Chicago, IL
Sherman Jackson, Assoc. Professor of Islamic Studies	University of Michigan, Ann Arbor, MI
Joyce King, Assistant Provost	Medgar Evers College-CUNY, Brooklyn, NY
Salahuddin Malik, Professor of History	State University of New York, Brockport, NY
Afaf L. Marsot, Professor Emeritus (History)	University of California, Los Angeles, CA
Ali A. Mazrui, Director-Inst. of Global Cultural Studies	State University of New York, Binghamton, NY
Aminah McCloud, Assoc. Professor of Islamic Studies	DePaul University, Chicago, IL
Akbar Muhammad, Assoc. Professor of History	State University of New York, Binghamton, NY
Azim Nanji, Director	Institute of Ismaili Studies, London, U.K.
Seyyed Hossein Nasr, Professor of Islamic Studies	George Washington University, Washington, D.C.
Sulayman S. Nyang, Professor of African Studies	Howard University, Washington, D.C.
Azade-Ayse Rorlich, Professor of History	University of Southern California, Los Angeles, CA
Muzammil H. Siddiqi, Adjunct Professor of Religion	California State University, Fullerton, CA
Dilnawaz A. Siddiqui, Professor of Communications	Clarion University, Clarion, PA

Office Address: 9300 Gardenia Avenue #B-3 Fountain Valley, CA 92708
Mailing Address: P.O. Box 20186 Fountain Valley, CA 92728-0186
tel: 714-839-2929 • fax: 714-839-2714
website: www.cie.org • e-mail: info@cie.org

Contributors

Barbara Allen	Orange Co. Dept. of Education, CA
Susan Douglass	Falls Church, VA
Tasneema Ghazi, Ph.D.	Iqra Intl. Education Foundation, Chicago, IL
Semeen Issa	Los Angeles Unified School District, CA
Freda Shamma, Ph.D.	Cincinnati, OH
Zeba Siddiqui	Fort Collins, CO
Catherine Young	Banning Unified School District, CA

Academic Reviewers

Karima-Diane Alavi • 10th Grade History Teacher
The Sidwell Friends School, Washington D.C.

Minhaj Arastu • World History Teacher
Irmo High School, Columbia, SC

Juan C. Contreras • Teacher
Spurgon Middle School, Santa Ana, CA

John Costa • World History and Chicano Studies Teacher
Arlington High School, Riverside, CA

Rkia E. Cornell, Ph.D. • Asst. Professor of Arabic - Dept. of Asian and African Languages & Literature
Duke University, Durham, NC

Connie DeCapite • Training Coordinator - Fullerton Intl. Resources for Schools and Teachers (FIRST)
California State University, Fullerton, CA

Ross Dunn, Ph.D. • Professor of History- Dept. of History
California State University, San Diego, CA

Shaker El-Sayed, Ph.D. • Director - Islamic Schools Dept.
Islamic Society of North America, Plainfield, IN

Carl W. Ernst, Ph.D. • Professor and Chair - Dept. of Religious Studies
University of North Carolina, Chapel Hill, NC

Eugene Geno Flores • Project Director, Center for the Study of Evaluation
University of California, Los Angeles, CA

Rosalind Ward Gwynne, Ph.D. • Assoc. Professor of Arabic and Islamic Studies - Dept. of Religious Studies
University of Tennessee, Knoxville, TN

Zayn Kassam Hann, Ph.D. • Asst. Professor of Religious Studies- Dept. of Religious Studies
Pomona College, Claremont, CA

Loretta J. Hannum • Curriculum Coordinator for Social Studies
Williamsburg - James City County Public Schools, VA

H. Michael Hartoonian, Ph.D. • President - National Council for the Social Studies, and
Professor - Graduate School, Hamline University, St. Paul, MN

Jo Marie Hayes • Teacher and Department Chair - Humanities
Costa Mesa High School, Costa Mesa, CA

Sandra Jackson, Ph.D. • Assoc. Professor of Education - School of Education
DePaul University, Chicago, IL

Tazim R. Kassam, Ph.D. • Asst. Professor of Islamic Studies and Religion - Dept. of Religion
Middlebury College, Middlebury, VT

Charles Kloes • Past Chair - California History-Social Science Curriculum Commission, and
History Teacher - Beverly Hills High School, Beverly Hills, CA

Richard F. Kraft • Chair - Social Studies Dept.
Los Altos High School, Hacienda Heights, CA

Judy Kraft • Instructor - Elementary Education
California State University, Fullerton, CA

Penelope Maguire • Seventh Grade Social Studies Teacher
Apex Middle School, Apex, NC

Shafia Mir • Graduate Student, Political Economy
University of Southern California, Los Angeles, CA

Louisa Moffitt • Southeast Regional Middle East and Islamic Studies Seminar (SERMEISS), and
Middle East Studies Teacher - Marist School, Atlanta, GA

John Parcels, Ph.D. • Professor - Dept. of English and Philosophy
Georgia Southern University, Stateboro, GA

Lynne Parrott • Teacher - Middle School Gifted Students
Richmond Hill Middle School, Richmond Hill, GA

Ken Perkins, Ph.D. • Professor of History - Dept. of History
University of South Carolina, Columbia, SC

Nicholas Piediscalzi, Ph.D. • Director - California Three Rs Project
Goleta, CA

Denny Schilling • Past-President - National Council for the Social Studies, and
Teacher, Social Studies - Homewood-Flossmoor High School, Flossmoor, IL

Agin Shaheed • Pupil Advocate, San Diego City Schools,
San Diego, CA

Linda Symcox, Ph.D. • Assoc. Director - National Center for History in the Schools
University of California, Los Angeles, CA

Mae Ussery • Instructor - Academy Program
Valley High School, Santa Ana, CA

Jonathan Weil, Ph.D. • Director - Western International Studies Consortium (WISC)
Immaculate Heart College, Los Angeles, CA

John Alden Williams, Ph.D. • Professor of Humanities in Religion - Dept. of Religion
College of William and Mary, Williamsburg, VA

Religious Reviewer

Muzammil Siddiqi, Ph.D. • Adjunct Professor of Religion
California State University, Fullerton, CA

From the Director...

Thank you for your interest in our third edition of the popular *Teaching About Islam and Muslims in the Public School Classroom*. As an educational organization, the Council on Islamic Education endeavors to provide the necessary resources for teachers to fulfill their commendable, and challenging, goal of educating our nation's students. Teaching about religion is especially difficult for many, and this problem is compounded by the fact that few resources exist for covering Islam in a more than superficial manner. This handbook has been prepared keeping this in mind, and in response to the fact that most state curricula call for "teaching about religions" and their role in human history. We hope this resource will also be a useful tool for educators wanting to broaden their multicultural horizons. In this edition, you'll find

- ❂ Expanded information on Muslim beliefs and practices, with more charts.

- ❂ Revised, comprehensive glossary of terms related to Islam, with pronunciation guide.

- ❂ Expanded and rewritten section on sensitivity-related matters and needs of Muslim students in the public school setting.

- ❂ Updated annotated list of recommended books, video tapes, teaching resources, and student reading materials.

We welcome input and suggestions from teachers, curriculum specialists, and other education professionals in order to continue providing needed resources in the future. We also invite educators to help the Council develop such tools and resources for teaching about Islam and Muslims in the public school classroom.

Please do let us know what you think of this latest effort.

As-salaam Alaykum (peace be unto you),

Shabbir Mansuri
Founding Director

Foreword

One of the most challenging responsibilities that teachers face today is the imparting of sensitive, unbiased, and historically accurate instruction related to religion. Not many of us were ready to face this challenge when the *California History/Social Science Framework* was adopted in 1987 and targeted specific objectives for such instruction. As the *Framework* asked us to use more authentic documents in our teaching and to bring out the "story" in history, we found ourselves with neither time nor resources to make this happen in our classrooms. Through years of struggling, discussing, searching and a great deal of learning, we now feel fairly comfortable with most of the innovations suggested in the *Framework*, except one—information and instruction related to religions.

Compounding our frustration in addressing religions in our classrooms, our student population is increasingly more diverse. Coming into our schools from many cultures, languages, educational backgrounds, and religious experiences—or lack thereof—our students look to us to impart not only American culture and history, but also a meaningful and accurate representation of their own cultural heritage, history and religion as well. Most of us feel ill-prepared to meet this challenge. This handbook for educators, prepared by the Council on Islamic Education, is both a helpful guide and a sensitive, accurate document written to enable us to meet the challenge of addressing one specific religion in our classrooms. Written by and about Muslims, this handbook is intended to explain Islam in ways that not only teachers, but students also, can understand. It includes four equally important and critical sections: information on Islam, discussion of sensitivity issues, recommended resources, and an extensive glossary. In addition, CIE has produced a number of teaching units that provide teachers with lessons and activities and black-line masters for teaching about Muslim and world history. The authors of these materials have long been frequent visitors and speakers in Orange County classrooms, enabling them to have a clear picture of their audience. Their positions in the Muslim community enable them to know the unique needs of Muslim students and the issues that the students and their parents feel are of importance for educators.

This handbook, then, not only helps teachers understand and teach about Islam to all our students, it also help us relate more effectively to our Muslim students and their families. Dr. Martin Luther King Jr., in his famous 1963 "I Have A Dream" speech, talked about "my people who stand on the warm threshold which leads into the palace of justice." Indeed, possibly the last barrier to the "palace of justice" lies in our lack of understanding and tolerance of religions other than our own. It is through materials such as this handbook for educators that we can celebrate our diversity, eliminate stereotypes, and build respect for our fellow humans. I am convinced that access to the door to Dr. King's palace lies in the hands of our teachers. How fitting it is, then, that this handbook is a product of both a religious community and an educational community, uniting to be stronger than either community alone, uniting to celebrate and learn from our diversity, uniting to make our classrooms a palace of justice.

Barbara L. Allen, Director of Program Delivery
California School Leadership Academy at Orange County
Orange County Dept. of Education, Costa Mesa, CA

Contents

Teaching with Sensitivity 53

Recommended Resources 73

Quick Reference Glossary 103

About Islam and Muslims

INTRODUCTION

What is Islam?

The term *Islam* derives from the three-letter Arabic root *s-l-m*, which generates words with interrelated meanings, including "surrender," "submission," "commitment" and "peace." Commonly, *Islam* refers to the monotheistic religion revealed to Muhammad ibn (son of) Abdullah between 610 and 632 of the common era. The name *Islam* was instituted by the *Qur'an*, the sacred scripture revealed to Muhammad. For believers, Islam is not a new religion. Rather, it represents the last reiteration of the primordial message of God's Oneness, a theme found in earlier monotheistic religious traditions.

Though Islam can be described as a religion, it is viewed by its adherents in much broader terms. Beyond belief in specific doctrines and performance of important ritual acts, Islam is practiced as a complete and natural way of life, designed to bring God into the center of one's consciousness, and thus one's life. Essentially, by definition Islam is a worldview focused on belief in the One God and commitment to His commandments.

What does the term "Allah" mean?

The Arabic word *Allah* is a contraction of the words "al" and "ilah," and literally means "The God." Believers in Islam understand *Allah* to be the proper name for the Creator as found in the *Qur'an*. The name *Allah* is analogous to *Eloh*, a Semitic term found in the divine scriptures revealed to Muhammad's predecessors Moses and Jesus (may peace be upon them all).

The use of the term *Allah* is not confined to believers in Islam alone — Arabic-speaking Christians and Jews also use *Allah* in reference to God, demonstrating thereby that followers of Islam, Christianity, and Judaism believe in a common monotheistic Creator, a fact that many people are surprised to learn. One reason for this may be that English-speaking persons are accustomed to the term *God*, whereas believers in Islam, regardless of their native language, use the Arabic word *Allah*. This difference in usage may cause people to view the term *Allah* with reticence and uncertainty, preventing them from making the connection between the Arabic name and the accepted English equivalent term. In other words, *Allah* means "God," like *Dios* and *Dieu* mean "God" in Spanish and French, respectively.

Who are Muslims?

The word *Muslim*, like *Islam*, comes from the three-letter Arabic root *s-l-m*, and literally means *"one who willfully submits (to God)."* Islam teaches that everything in Creation — microbes, plants, animals, mountains and rivers, planets, and so forth — is "muslim," testifying to the majesty of the Creator and submitting or committing to His divine laws. Human beings, also, are considered fundamentally "muslim" (submitters to God) in their original spiritual orientation, but being unique creations endowed with abilities of reason, judgement, and choice, they may remain on a God-conscious, righteous path towards divine reward, or may veer away as a consequence of upbringing and life-choices.

More commonly, the term *Muslim* refers to one who believes in the *Shahadah* (the declaration of faith containing the basic creed of Islam) and embraces a lifestyle in accord with Islamic principles and values. Anybody may be or become a Muslim, regardless of gender, race, nationality, color, or social or economic status. A non-Muslim who decides to enter Islam does so by reciting the *Shahadah*, (pronounced *La-Ilaha Ila Allah, Muhammad-un Rasool Allah*) witnessing that "there is no deity but *Allah* (God), and Muhammad is His Messenger."

Where do Muslims live throughout the world?

Over 1.3 billion people throughout the world are adherents of Islam. In other words, one out of every five human beings on the planet is a Muslim. Islam is the religion of diverse peoples living in Europe, Africa, the Middle East, Central, East, South and Southeast Asia, Japan, Australia, and North and South America. The global spectrum of races, ethnicities and cultures finds representation in the worldwide Muslim community.

While Islam is often associated almost exclusively with the Middle East, Arabs comprise only about 15-18% of all Muslims. Interestingly, the country with the largest population of Muslims (over 170 million) is Indonesia, an island nation in Southeast Asia. Furthermore, the Muslim peoples of the South Asian subcontinent (living in Pakistan, India, Bangladesh, and Sri Lanka) constitute about 25% of all Muslims, while those of Africa comprise close to 20% of the total. Surprisingly to some, there are nearly as many Muslims in China as there are in Iran, Egypt or Turkey (over 50 million). Moreover, Muslims constitute sizeable minorities in many Western European countries, including England (over 2 million), France (over 2 million - about 10% of the French population), and Germany (about 2 million). See the chart on the following page for more details.

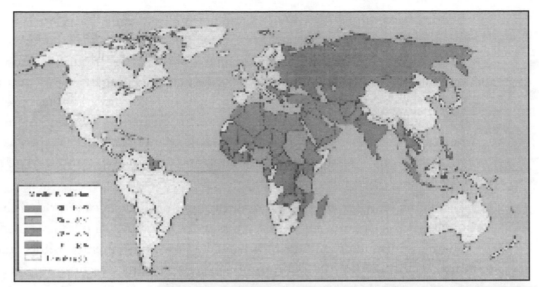

Do Muslims share a single culture?

Muslims throughout the world share the same essential beliefs, values, and God-centered approach to the world. Furthermore, all Muslims look to the *Qur'an* and the lifestyle and traditions of Prophet Muhammad for guidance in their daily affairs. In this respect, since Muslims the world over try to implement *Qur'anic* and Prophetic guidance, it may be said that Muslims share a common Islamic culture, focusing on shared principles and values. As a result, Muslims typically feel at home among their co-religionists anywhere in the world.

The Worldwide Muslim Population

Country or Region	Est. Population	Percentage
South Asia (Pakistan, India, Bangladesh)	275 million	23%
Africa	200 million	16.7%
Arab Countries	180 million	15%
Southeast Asia (Indonesia, Malaysia, Singapore…)	170 million	14.2%
Central Asia	50 million	4.2%
China	50 million	4.2%
Iran	50 million	4.2%
Turkey	50 million	4.2%
Europe	20 million	1.7%
Afghanistan	15 million	1.3%
North America	6 million	0.5%
South America	3 million	0.25%
Australia	1 million	0.08%
other areas	130 million	10.5%
Total	1,200,000,000	100%

Sources:
Fareed Numan, American Muslim Council, Washington D.C. (1992)
Islamic Affairs Dept., Embassy of Saudi Arabia, Washington D.C.
World Almanac (1995)

At the same time, the ethnic, regional or material cultures of Muslims vary tremendously across the globe. Muslims exhibit different styles of clothing, different tastes for food and drink, diverse languages, and varying traditions and customs. American Muslims fall within this panorama and are in many ways culturally distinct from Muslims living in other societal contexts. Little League baseball, apple pie, and jazz music are as natural to American Muslims as they are to other Americans. Even so, certain aspects of popular American culture (such as pre-marital relations, comsumption of alcohol, and certain styles of dress) do not accord with Islamic principles.

Muslims view the diversity found throughout the *ummah* (worldwide Muslim community) as a natural part of God's plan for humanity and believe it contributes to Islam's continued vitality and universal ethos. Consequently, rather than imposing arbitrary cultural uniformity, diverse cultural practices are encouraged and supported. So long as a given cultural practice or tradition does not violate teachings of Islam as found in the *Qur'an* and traditions of Prophet Muhammad, it is considered legitimate and possibly even beneficial. Using this approach, Muslims throughout history have been able to retain in large part their own distinct cultures, discarding only those elements contrary to the basic moral and ethical principles of Islam.

How many Muslims live in the United States?

An estimated five to seven million Muslims live in North America, and of these, over two and a half million are Americans who have embraced Islam (i.e. they were not born into the faith). Dr. John R. Weeks, Director of the International Population Center, San Diego State University, a noted demographer and author, states: "There can be no question that the Muslim population in this country is large and is growing at a fairly rapid pace." It is projected that by the turn of the century, Islam will be the second largest religion in the United States. Even today, Muslims outnumber Episcopalians, Lutherans, Presbyterians, the United Church of Christ and many other Christian denominations, and almost as many Muslims as Jews call America their home.

The United States Department of Defense reports that there are currently more than 9,000 Muslims on active duty in the U.S. armed services. A number of leading American scientists, physicians, sports figures, and scholars are Muslim. Clearly, Muslims are part of the diverse fabric of the United States, playing a productive role in our society as neighbors, co-workers, colleagues, schoolmates, and friends. Most American Muslims share in the effort to make this nation, as well as the world, a more moral, just and peaceful place in which to live, worship and prosper.

What is the Muslim community in North America like?

Muslims from various walks of life live in every state of the union. The ten states with the largest Muslim populations, listed in order, are California, New York, Illinois, New Jersey, Indiana, Michigan, Virginia, Texas, Ohio, and Maryland. Muslims in these ten states constitute 3.3 million (more than 50%) of the American Muslim population.

The Muslim Population of North America		
Ethnic Group or Origin	Est. Population	Percentage
African-American	2,100,000	42.0%
South Asian	1,220,000	24.4%
Arab	620,000	12.4%
African	260,000	5.2%
Iranian	180,000	3.6%
Turkic	120,000	2.4%
Southeast Asian	100,000	2.0%
Euro-American	80,000	1.6%
East European	40,000	0.8%
Undetermined	280,000	5.6%
Total	5,000,000	100%

Source:
Fareed Numan, American Muslim Council, Washington D.C. (1992)

There are more than 1,200 *masjids* (mosques) throughout the United States, as well as over 400 Islamic schools (126 full-time), three colleges, 400 associations, an estimated 200,000 businesses, and over 200 publications, journals, and weekly newspapers.

The number of houses of worship serves as one measure of the growth of the Muslim community in the United States. In 1930, there were 19 *masjids* in America. By 1960 there were more than 230; by 1980 over 600; and as noted above, by 1995 over 1,200.

The diversity of Muslims in the United States is a hallmark of the community — virtually every race, ethnicity and culture is represented among American Muslims, making for a unique experience not found anywhere else in the world.

What is the history of Islam in America?

The history of Islam in the New World in some sense precedes that of the United States itself. Some researchers claim that certain artifacts, found in the Mississippi delta and other locales, antedating the European "voyages of discovery," lend credence to the possibility of Arab or African expeditions into the as-then-uncharted Ocean Sea, as the Atlantic Ocean was commonly known. Arab scientists and astronomers knew the earth to be round long before the concept gained currency in European circles. When it did, European sailing vessels, including those under Christopher Columbus' command, that crossed the Atlantic in search of an alternate passage to Asia often enlisted Muslim crew members, due to their expertise in maritime navigation. Also, since European explorers, who spoke little Arabic, expected to reach India (hence the term "Indian" for Native Americans) and the Indian Ocean basin (where Arabs were heavily involved in maritime trade and commerce), taking along Arabs/Muslims as translators made sense.

Milestones in American Muslim History	
1500s	Arrival of Hispano-Arab Muslims (Mudejars) from Spain in Spanish-occupied territories of the New World.
1539	Moroccan guide Estephan participated in exploration of Arizona and New Mexico for the viceroy of New Spain.
1717	Arrival of enslaved Africans who professed belief in Allah and Prophet Muhammad and curiously (to their captives) refused to eat pork.
1856	Hajji Ali hired by United States cavalry to experiment in raising camels in Arizona.
1869	A number of Yemenis arrived after the opening of the Suez Canal in Egypt.
1908	Muslim immigrants from Syria, Lebanon, Jordan, other Arab lands.
1922	Islamic Association formed in Detroit, Michigan.
1933	Nation of Islam formed.
1934	First building designated as a masjid established in Cedar Rapids, Iowa.
1952	Muslim servicemen allowed to identify their religion as Islam by Federal government.
1963	Muslim Students' Association (MSA) founded.
1965	El-Hajj Malik El-Shabazz (Malcolm X) assassinated in New York.
1975	Warith Deen Muhammad renounced teachings of Nation of Islam and led large segment of African-American community into mainstream Islam.
1982	Islamic Society of North America (ISNA) formed.
1983	Islamic College founded in Chicago, Illinois.
1991	Imam Siraj Wahhaj of Brooklyn, New York offered the invocation to the United States House of Representatives.
1991	Charles Bilal became the first Muslim mayor of an American city, Kountze, Texas.
1992	Imam Warith Deen Muhammad offered the invocation to the United States Senate.
1993	The first Muslim chaplain is hired by the United States Armed Forces.
1993	Islamic Shura Council, a coalition of four major Muslim organizations, established.

Sources:
A Century of Islam in America (Yvonne Haddad, 1986)
American Muslim Council (1992)

Later on in American history, during the eighteenth and nineteenth centuries, as many as 20% of the slaves brought to the United States from Africa were Muslims (before being forcibly converted to Christianity). Another group of Muslims, Spaniards known as *Mudejars*, established roots in the New World after the conquest of Granada in 1492 and the expulsion of Muslims and Jews from Spain resulting from the Inquisition. The influence of these highly-skilled Hispano-Arab Muslim craftsmen and artists has had far-reaching effects in American architecture and design, which are still in evidence today, especially in the American Southwest.

In the modern era, since the late 1800s, Muslims from all over the world, along with people of other faiths, have immigrated to the U.S. to make a better life for themselves and to contribute their unique talents and sensibilities to the ever-evolving American social matrix. In the last fifty years, a dramatic increase in native-born American Muslims and converts to Islam has taken place as well, providing new generations of Muslims prepared to interact fruitfully with fellow Americans and raise the contributions of the community to higher levels.

BASIC BELIEFS

What are the beliefs of Muslims?

The central concept in Islam, reflected in the *Shahadah*, is *tawheed*, or Oneness of God. For Muslims, there is but One God who is Lord and Sovereign of Creation, and devotion, allegiance, and obedience must first of all be to Him. This view serves as the foundation from which the basic beliefs of Islam emanate, since God is recognized as *the* Source for all knowledge and understanding. More specifically, the beliefs of Muslims are delineated and described in the *Qur'an* and in the sayings and traditions of Prophet Muhammad. The practice of Islam is based upon belief in One God (*Allah*), creations (whether humanly perceivable or not) of God, prophetic leadership, revealed guidance, and a Day of Judgement. Details are provided below.

Is there a Judeo-Christian-Islamic tradition?

Important doctrinal differences exist between Judaism, Christianity and Islam. Even so, each of the three faiths proceed from a monotheistic worldview interconnected with that of the other two. The three world religions share belief in successive prophets and revealed scriptures — in fact, the three faiths trace their religious history back to the patriarch Abraham, and earlier to the first human, Adam (considered a prophet in Islam), demonstrating a common history and outlook. Thus, for Muslims Islam culminates what can be described as the *Judeo-Christian-Islamic* tradition of monotheism.

ALLAH

How is God viewed in Islam?

Basic Beliefs of Muslims	
Muslims believe in...	
Allah	The One God
Angels	(and the world of the Unseen)
Prophets	(and Muhammad as the final prophet)
Divine Scriptures	(and the Qur'an as the final scripture)
Day of Judgement	(and reward in Heaven and punishment in Hell)

The *Qur'an*, the divinely-revealed scripture of Islam, contains numerous verses describing the nature of God. The role of human beings as creations of God upon the earth and their relationship with God are also discussed extensively in the sacred text.

"Say: He is God, the One, the Eternal, Absolute. He does not beget, nor is He begotten, and there is none like unto Him." (Qur'an, 112:1-4)

"It is He who brought you forth from the wombs of your mothers when you knew nothing, and He gave you hearing and sight and intelligence and affections that you may give thanks." (Qur'an, 16:78)

"No vision can grasp Him, but His grasp is over all vision. He is above all comprehension, yet is acquainted with all things." (Qur'an, 6:103)

Muslims believe that God has no partners or associates who share in His divinity or authority. Muslims also believe that God is transcendent and unlike His creations, and thus has no physical form. Nor is God believed to exist in (or be represented by) any material object. A number of divine attributes or "names," which serve to describe God, are found in the *Qur'an*. Some commonly known attributes include the Most Merciful, the Most Forgiving, the Most High, the Unique, and the Everlasting, among others.

In Islam, human beings, like other creations, are seen as completely unlike God, though they may aspire to exhibit various attributes manifested by God, such as justice or mercy. Furthermore, even while God is believed to be beyond traditional human perception, the *Qur'an* states *"He is with you wherever you may be"* (57:5). For Muslims, God's Oneness heightens the awareness that ultimately all life is bound by Divine Law emanating from a singular source and that life has a meaning and purpose which revolves around the consciousness of God's presence.

Moreover, belief in a singular Creator compels conscientious Muslims to view all humanity as one extended family, and treat others with justice and equity. Respect for the environment and natural resources also follows from the Muslim view of God.

ANGELS

How do Muslims view Angels?

Mala'ikah, or Angels, are believed to be among God's many creations, and belief in angels is symbolic of a Muslim's belief in *al-Ghayb*, the world of the unseen (a world of which only God has knowledge). Angels are considered heavenly beings created by God to perform various duties. Angels by nature do not deviate from righteousness, as they do not possess an inherent free will as do human beings.

Some angels are considered more prominent than others. *Jibreel* (Gabriel), for example, is known as the "Angel of Revelation," since he communicated God's revelations and scriptures to various human prophets. He also announced (much to her surprise and incredulity) to Mary, mother of Jesus, that she would bear the Messiah awaited by the Children of Israel. Indeed, *Jibreel* is uniquely described in the *Qur'an* as a Spirit (*ruh*) from God due to his role in bridging the divine and human spheres.

Muslims also believe that each human being is assigned two angels by God—one to keep track of good deeds, and the other to record bad deeds or sins. Tradition holds that these "personal" angels will present the records of one's deeds to each individual as he or she stands before God on the Day of Judgement.

Is Satan a "fallen" angel?

Most commentators of the *Qur'anic* account of Creation do not view Satan as a fallen angel. Rather, he is believed to be one of the *jinn*, a class of God's creation distinct from angels. The *jinn*, like angels, exist in the unseen world, and cannot ordinarily be perceived by human beings. Like humans, however, the *jinn* have been endowed with free will, and thus can choose to act according to God's commands.

When God commanded *Iblis* (the personal name of Satan), a leader among the *jinn*, to bow before Adam in recognition of human eminence among God's creations, he rebelled and was cast out with his followers. Iblis asked God for a respite until the Day of Judgement to prove that he could undermine humankind's claim to superiority. A recurrent theme in all of God's revelations to humanity is that of Satan's machinations against humankind. The *Qur'an* repeatedly warns against deviating from the "straight path" by falling prey to Satan's temptations. Satan has no independent source of power over humans—only what they cede to him.

PROPHETS

What is the role of prophets in Islam?

Muslims believe that God has provided guidance to humanity over the ages through the institution of prophethood. In the Islamic context, prophets are not persons who prophesy (foretell the future); rather they are seen as righteous and truthful messengers selected by God to fulfill the most important mission—calling on people to worship God alone, and teaching them to live righteously, in accordance with God's commandments. Muslims believe prophets, and the scriptures given to some of them, are the only sure sources of God's guidance, and that God has chosen, throughout history, thousands of prophets from among all peoples of the earth, culminating with the last prophet, Muhammad.

> *"Say: We believe in Allah and that which is revealed to us, and in what was revealed to Abraham, Ishmael, Isaac, Jacob, and the tribes, to Moses and Jesus and the other prophets from their Lord. We make no distinction between any of them, and to Allah we have surrendered ourselves." (Qur'an, 2:136)*

Some Prophets of Islam

Arabic Name	English Name
Adam	Adam
Nuh	Noah
Ibrahim	Abraham
Isma'il	Ishmael
Is-haq	Isaac
Yacoob	Jacob
Musa	Moses
Haroon	Aaron
Dawood	David
Sulayman	Solomon
Yahya	John
Isa	Jesus
Muhammad	Muhammad

Thus, in Islam, the prophets are seen as spiritual brothers one to another. Some commonly known figures who are considered prophets in Islam include Noah, Jonah, Abraham, Ishmael, Isaac, Joseph, Moses, David, Solomon, and Jesus. The chain of prophethood ended with Muhammad (570-632 C.E.), who lived 600 years after his predecessor Jesus.

Essentially, prophets give warnings as well as glad tidings to fellow human beings: warnings of punishment in this world and the next for unjust, immoral people who have turned away from God and His natural order, and glad tidings of reward in this world and the next for those who are conscious of God and follow His guidance as revealed to the prophets.

The *Qur'an* mentions twenty-five prophets by name, and tradition indicates that many thousands of prophets were chosen by God throughout human history between the time of Adam and that of Muhammad.

Do Muslims believe in Adam & Eve? How about "Original Sin"?

Adam and *Hawwa* (the Arabic name for Eve) are believed to be the first human beings, endowed by God with faculties not found in other earthly creatures. Furthermore, the *Qur'an* indicates that the first souls of man and woman originated from a single soul cleft in two, demonstrating the spiritual coequality of men and women.

The blissful Garden in which Adam and Hawwa initially dwelt proved to be a testing ground as well. God had warned the two not to eat of the fruit from a particular tree, yet at the insistence of Iblis (Satan), the two succumbed to temptation. Realizing that they had transgressed against God, the two repented and were ultimately forgiven. Thereafter, God placed the two on earth and multiplied the human race in order to test humanity and give humans the opportunity to demonstrate their highest potential in the face of continued temptation from Satan and his minions.

According to the *Qur'anic* account, both Adam and Eve sinned equally when they disobeyed God's command to stay clear of the forbidden tree; Eve does not figure as a temptress leading to "man's downfall." Furthermore, since God assigns every individual his or her freedom and responsibilities, Muslims do not believe in "Original Sin," the concept that the sin of Adam is inherited by all humankind. Rather, Muslims believe that each person is personally accountable to God, and will be judged by Him according to their good and bad deeds, independent of those of others.

> *"Those who believe and work righteous deeds, from them shall We blot out all evil, and We shall reward them according to the best of their deeds."* (Qur'an, 29:7)

What is Islam's view of Jesus?

Muslims believe that Jesus was a very important prophet of God, and that he was indeed the Messiah awaited by the Jews of ancient Palestine. Like Christians, Muslims believe Jesus' mission was to reestablish justice among people and rectify deviations that had developed in the religion of the One God. Muslims share with Christians belief in Jesus' unique birth and various miracles performed by him (by God's leave).

> *"Lo! The angels said: 'O Mary! Behold, God sends thee the glad tiding, through a word from Him, of a son who shall become known as the Christ Jesus, son of Mary, of great honour in this world and in the life to come, and of those who are drawn near to God."* (Qur'an, 3:45)

However, Muslims do not believe in Jesus' divinity, and do not consider Jesus the "Son of God," for to do so would contradict the *Qur'anic* concept of God's Unity (Oneness). Furthermore, since the concept of "Original Sin" does not exist in Islam, neither Jesus nor any other prophet or person plays a redemptive role in human salvation. In other words, there is no concept of "vicarious atonement" in Islam. Moreover, Muslims do not share the Christian belief in Jesus' crucifixion. According to the *Qur'an*, Jesus was assumed (taken up) to the realm of God to spare him such a fate.

In the *Qur'an*, God's creation of Jesus, who had no father, is likened to His creation of Adam, who had neither father nor mother. Both, fashioned out of earth's elemental components, are viewed as direct manifestations of God's Divine Command "Be!"

Who was Muhammad?

History records that a person by the name Muhammad was born into the tribe of Quraysh in the city of Makkah in 570 C.E. His father, Abdullah, died before his birth. When Muhammad was six years old, his mother, Amina became ill and died. Thus, at a very young age Muhammad experienced the loss of his parents and became an orphan.

For the next few years Muhammad was entrusted to his grandfather, Abd al-Muttalib. When Muhammad was eight years old, his grandfather also passed away. His uncle Abu Talib, a well-respected member of the Quraysh tribe, took responsibility for him. Muhammad grew up to become an honest and trustworthy businessman. Indeed, Muhammad's upright and dependable reputation earned him the designation *al-Amin* ("the Trustworthy One") among his fellow Makkans, and even invited a marriage proposal from Khadijah, a businesswoman in Makkah for whom Muhammad worked.

At the age of twenty-five, Muhammad married Khadijah, a widow who was his elder by fifteen years. Their marriage lasted twenty-five years, until Khadijah's death. Muhammad and Khadijah had six children: two sons died in early childhood, and four daughters lived to bless their household.

While most of his fellow Makkans were polytheists, Muhammad refused to worship the traditional tribal deities and often retreated to meditate and worship the One God of his ancestor, Abraham. At the age of forty, while meditating in the cave of Hira in the mountains above Makkah, Muhammad received the first of many revelations, beginning with the Arabic word *Iqra*, meaning "Read" or "Recite." Soon afterwards, he was commanded to convey the Divine message and thus became the last messenger of God, according to the *Qur'an*.

"Read, in the name of thy Lord, Who Created—
Created man, out of a clot (embryo).
Proclaim! And thy Lord is Most Bountiful,
He Who taught the use of the pen—
Taught man that which he knew not." (Qur'an, 96:1-5)

Muhammad spent the remaining twenty-three years of his life receiving revelations from God and advocating the message of Islam among the peoples of the Arabian peninsula and working to implement the principles and teachings of Islam in human society. After suffering severe persecution from the polytheistic Makkans for 11 years, he and his fellow Muslims emigrated to Yathrib, a city 200 miles north of Makkah, where he established Islamic rule. The city was renamed *Madinah* (short for *Madinat an-Nabi*, City of the Prophet). In the following years, the message of Islam brought more and more tribes in the Arabian peninsula into the fold, creating a new community based on common religious principles, rather than tribal or other affiliations. Muhammad died in 632 C.E. at the age of 63. His tomb is located adjacent to the *Masjid an-Nabawi* (Prophet's Masjid) in Madinah, Saudi Arabia, in what used to be his quarters next to the original *masjid* of the city.

What was Muhammad's role as the last prophet?

Islam teaches that Muhammad's role as the final prophet of God was to confirm the authentic teachings of previous prophets and to rectify mistakes or innovations that followers of previous monotheistic faith traditions had introduced into the original religion of humankind. Muhammad is also viewed as the conduit for the completion of God's guidance to humanity; the scope of his mission is seen as encompassing all people, rather than a specific region, group or community. Furthermore, his life serves as a perfect model of how to practice Islam fully.

"We have sent you forth to all humankind, so that you may give them
good news and warn them." (Qur'an, 34:28)

Muslims believe that the original revelations or scriptures given by God to prophets such as Abraham, Moses, David, and Jesus had been lost or modified over time. Moreover, the ethno-religious concept of a "chosen people" found in Judaism and the doctrines of Trinity and Original Sin found in Christianity are believed to be later developments that grew away from the original practices and scriptures of previous prophets.

Essentially, Muslims view Islam not as a "new" religion, since it embodies the same message and guidance that God revealed to all His messengers, but rather a reestablishment of the "primordial" religion of humankind, centered around recognizing God's Oneness and adhering to His commands. The view of Islam as having achieved its final form through the scripture given to Muhammad and his own teachings is an important aspect of faith. Consequently, Muhammad is considered the final messenger of God, the "Seal" of the Prophets. Any claimants to prophethood after Muhammad, who died in 632 C.E., are not accepted by Muslims.

"Muhammad is the father of no man among you. He is the Apostle of Allah and the seal of the Prophets. Allah has knowledge of all things." (Qur'an, 33:40)

What is the "Sunnah" of Muhammad? What are "Hadith"?

The term *Sunnah* refers to the sayings and actions of Prophet Muhammad, as distinct from the revelations that comprise the *Qur'an*. It is the second source of Islam after the *Qur'an*, for in the Prophet there is a *"beautiful pattern of conduct for any whose hope is in God and the Last Day"* (Qur'an, 33:21).

Hadith – Sayings of Prophet Muhammad

- "Obey your parents and treat them kindly for if you do so then your own children will be obedient and kind to you."
- "Heaven lies under the feet of the mother."
- "All children are God's children and those dearest to God are those who treat His children kindly."
- "When three people are together two should not talk secretly, leaving the third alone, since this may grieve him."
- "Seeking knowledge is a duty of every Muslim."
- "Exchange presents with one another for they remove ill feelings from the heart."
- "Take advantage of five things before five others happen: your youth before you grow old; your health before you fall sick; your money before you become poor; your leisure before you become busy and your life before you die."
- "Cleanliness is half of the religion."
- "The most perfect in faith amongst Muslim men is he who is best in manner and kindest to his wife."
- "Powerful is not he who knocks the other down. Indeed powerful is he who controls himself when he is angry."
- "If one of you sees something evil he should change it with his hand. If he cannot he should speak out against it, and if he cannot do even that he should at least detest it in his heart."
- "Actions are judged according to their intentions, and every person will be judged (in the hereafter) according to what he or she intends."
- "The world is green and beautiful, and God has appointed you His stewards over it."
- "Modesty and Faith are joined closely together and if either of them is lost, the other goes also."
- "The best richness is the richness of the soul."
- "God will show no compassion on the one who has no compassion towards all humankind."
- "He who eats his fill while his neighbor goes without food is not a believer."

When the Prophet's wife Aisha was asked about her husband's character, she stated simply, "It was the *Qur'an*," meaning that his life was the *Qur'an* in application. Based on this premise, the Prophet is considered by all Muslims a guide and role model for living a successful life—one who emulates the Prophet receives God's mercy and forgiveness. Following Muhammad's example contributes to a Muslim's efforts to fulfill obligations to God and gain entrance into Paradise.

One form in which Muhammad's *Sunnah* has been recorded and preserved is the *Hadith* (traditions of the Prophet). Hadith are records of the doings and personal sayings of the Prophet. *Hadith* were painstakingly verified and compiled by scholars in various books in the centuries following the Prophet's death. Six collections of *hadith* are considered the most authentic, the most commonly used ones being the volumes titled *Sahih Bukhari* and *Sahih Muslim*.

Who were the Sahabah?

Before Muhammad's message arrived, Makkah had become a center of polytheistic practices and tribal affiliations dictated power and social relations. Many of the Quraysh opposed the Prophet's teachings, since his revolutionary message of social justice and equality undermined their sense of tradition, prosperity and tribal obligation. However, there were some who responded to the Prophet's call to righteousness and belief in the One God. Gradually, the number of Muslims grew. These individuals, who embraced Islam and who were close companions of Prophet Muhammad, are known as *Sahabah*.

Accounts from the lives of the *sahabah* (companions) are important as additional sources for proper behavior and practice. Many of the characteristics exhibited by various companions of the Prophet serve as inspiration to Muslims the world over. For example, the courage of Ali ibn Abi Talib sleeping in the Prophet's stead on the night the Quraysh planned to assassinate him reminds Muslims to challenge hostility or ill-will head-on, and the ingenuity of Salman al-Farsi, who recommended that the Muslims dig a deep trench around Madinah to thwart the forces of the Quraysh during one particular battle encourages Muslims to constantly seek novel solutions to seemingly insurmountable obstacles. And the selfless dedication and piety of Sumayyah bint Khubbat, who was killed by a Qurayshi notable for her newly adopted belief in Islam, thereby becoming the first martyr, is also well-remembered.

DIVINE SCRIPTURES

What is a "divinely revealed" scripture?

A divinely revealed scripture is a holy book or collection of writings believed to have divine, rather than human, origins. Muslims believe God revealed scriptures to certain prophets to communicate

Holy Scriptures of Islam		
Arabic Name	English Name	Prophet who received the scripture
Suhuf	Scrolls	Ibrahim (Abraham)
Tawrah	Torah	Musa (Moses)
Zabur	Psalms	Dawood (David)
Injeel	Evangelium	Isa (Jesus)
Qur'an	Qur'an	Muhammad

His commandments and guidance to humanity. For Muslims, belief in the original scriptures revealed to Abraham (Scrolls), Moses (Torah, including the Ten Commandments), David (Psalms) and Jesus (Evangelium or original Gospel) is an essential component of faith. Indeed, one cannot be considered a Muslim unless one believes in these previous scriptures and their historical role in the spiritual development of humankind.

How were divine scriptures revealed?

The angel or heavenly Spirit *Jibreel* (Gabriel) is believed to have transmitted divine communication from God to human prophets and personages (such as Mary, mother of Jesus). As such, Jibreel figures prominently in the history of scriptural revelation, culminating with the holy book revealed to Muhammad. In 610 C.E., at the age of 40, while in spiritual retreat in the cave of Hira above Makkah, Muhammad was visited by Jibreel for the first time. During this encounter, Jibreel revealed the first of many divine verses that would eventually comprise the *Qur'an*. Muslims believe God revealed His holy scriptures to the prophets in their native language. For this reason, the Torah was revealed to Moses in Hebrew, while the *Qur'an* was revealed to Muhammad in Arabic.

What is the Qur'an?

The word *Qur'an* literally means "the reading" or "the recitation," and refers to the divinely revealed scripture given to Muhammad. Since Muhammad is considered the last prophet of God, the *Qur'an* is believed to be the final revelation from God to humanity.

The *Qur'an* is considered by Muslims to be the literal Speech of God given to Muhammad in the Arabic language. The chapters and verses of the *Qur'an* were revealed throughout Prophet Muhammad's mission, over a span of close to twenty-three years, from 610-632 C.E. Contrary to common misconception, Muhammad is not the author of the *Qur'an*. Rather, he is viewed as the chosen transmitter of the revelation and the ideal implementor of principles and commandments contained therein. The personal sayings or words of Muhammad are known as *hadith*, which are distinct from the divine origin of the content of the *Qur'an*.

As verses of the *Qur'an* were revealed to Muhammad and subsequently repeated by him to companions and other fellow Muslims, they were written down, recited and memorized. The Prophet also typically led the formal worship five times daily, during which he recited the revealed verses according to the procedure that he established. The verses were also recited out loud by designated Muslims in the early dawn hours and prior to the worship times and other important occasions. In short, the *Qur'anic* verses played an immediate and practical role in the spiritual lives of Muslims from the outset. Before he passed away, the Prophet arranged the 114 chapters into the sequence we find in the *Qur'an*. Scholars, both Muslim and non-Muslim, agree that the *Qur'an* has remained intact and unchanged to the present. The *Qur'an* as a scripture stands unique in this regard.

Do translations of the Qur'an exist in other languages?

Translations of the *Qur'an* exist in many languages throughout the world, including English, Spanish, French, German, Urdu, Chinese, Malay, Vietnamese, and others. It is important to note that while translations are useful as renderings or explanations of the *Qur'an*, only the original Arabic text is considered to be the *Qur'an* itself. As a consequence, Muslims the world over, regardless of their native language, always strive to learn Arabic, so they can read and understand the *Qur'an* in its original form. Muslims also learn Arabic in order to recite the daily formal worship (*salah*) and for greeting one another with traditional expressions. However, while almost all Muslims have some basic familiarity with the Arabic language, not all Muslims speak fluent Arabic.

What is the structure and content of the Qur'an?

The *Qur'an* is comprised of 114 *surahs* (chapters) containing over six thousand *ayahs* (verses). The *surahs* were not arranged according to the sequence in which they were revealed; rather, they were arranged according to the Prophet's instructions, with the longest chapter (*al-Baqarah*, The Cow) near the beginning.

The various *surahs* discuss many of the same events and issues found in the Bible, but in a different fashion. Rather than presenting a sequential account of human spiritual history beginning with Adam and culminating with Muhammad, the *Qur'an's* chapters focus on various important themes and issues. In essence, the *Qur'an* was revealed as a book of guidance. In its own unique style it addresses a variety of subjects such as humans' relationship with God, His unique attributes, accountability and the Day of Judgement, ethics, social justice, politics, the rise and fall of nations, law, the natural world and family issues. The *Qur'an* stresses the development of certain moral and spiritual characteristics, and links these with establishing justice and righteousness in the world. Many of the lessons of the *Qur'an* are given through accounts of past prophets and their missions to their respective people.

Muslims also view the Qur'an as providing answers to questions such as: *What are the duties and responsibilities given to me by God? How should I interact with family, friends, colleagues, classmates, clients or customers, as well as other creations of God, even the environment? How should I treat myself as a human being endowed with a free will, the ability to reason and make choices, as well as various innate desires and drives?*

DAY OF JUDGEMENT

What is the Day of Judgement?

Muslims believe that our essential purpose in this world is to recognize and serve God by implementing His guidance as found in His divine scriptures. The role of prophets culminating with Muhammad has been to serve as role models for righteous behavior and warners of potential punishment for those who fail to heed God's commandments. Islam teaches that human beings are responsible to God for all their words and deeds. The relatively short span of our lives, therefore, constitutes a test.

> "He is the One who created death and life that He may test which of you is best in deeds." (Qur'an, 67:2).

> "Say: 'Behold my prayer, and (all) acts of my worship, and my living and my dying are for God (alone), the Sustainer of all the worlds.'" (Qur'an, 6:162).

In the interest of justice and to fulfill God's divine plan, a day will come when the present world will be destroyed and the entire human race will be resurrected and assembled before God for individual judgement. One will either be rewarded with permanent bliss in *Jannah* (Paradise) or be punished with suffering in *Jahannam* (Hell). However, the infinite mercy of God is demonstrated in the Qur'anic statement that those who have even a mustard seed's weight of belief in God will eventually be admitted into Heaven.

How is "salvation" viewed by Muslims?

For Muslims, following the straight path laid down by the prophets and exemplified by the last Prophet, Muhammad, whose message has been preserved since its revelation, is the means of safety and salvation. According to Muslim belief, a person who consciously rejects the prophets and their message is rejecting God, and thereby earns His wrath. Those who have not consciously rejected any prophet will be judged according to their belief in God and their good deeds. Ultimately, the Creator is the sole judge, and Muslims believe that no human being can judge another in spiritual terms. A *hadith* states: *"A person may appear to be working the deeds of the people of Paradise, while he is among the people of the Fire. And a person may appear to be working the deeds of the people of the Fire, while he is among the people of Paradise."*

For Muslims, belief in accountability to God and responsibility for one's own deeds gives one a sense of purpose, and every moment and event in life has religious purport. Thus, awareness of God's presence serves as a deterrent against crime, corruption, immorality and injustice as well as a means of acknowledging the role of God in one's life.

What is the Muslim view of the Afterlife?

Muslims believe that death is not the end of life, but rather a transitory state. After death, life continues in a different form. Various verses in the Qur'an describe Heaven as a place of blissful gardens and rivers, where all of one's desires may be fulfilled, while Hell is described as a place of fire and torment. Some scholars believe that such descriptions are in part allegorical, and serve to provide in human terms a symbol for the experience of the afterlife. Even so, no matter what form they take, physical or ethereal, reward and punishment are considered patently real by Muslims.

"O my devotees! No fear shall be on you that Day, nor shall you grieve. Tell those who believe in Our signs and surrender themselves: 'Enter the Garden rejoicing, both you and your spouses!' To them will be passed round dishes and goblets of gold; there they will have all that the souls could desire; all that the eyes could delight in; and you shall abide therein forever. Such will be the Garden of which you are made heirs for your good deeds in life." (Qur'an, 43:68-72)

"Those who reject Allah, for them will be the Fire of Hell; no term shall be determined for them, that they may die, nor shall its penalty be lightened for them; thus do We reward every ungrateful one."
(Qur'an, 35: 36)

RELIGIOUS OBLIGATIONS – THE FIVE PILLARS

What are the major religious obligations in Islam?

Every action performed in obedience to God's guidance or in order to please Him is considered an act of *ibadah* (worship) in Islam. Thus, helping someone with their homework, greeting a stranger, or even hugging one's spouse are at the same time acts of worship which earn spiritual reward. However, it is the specific acts of worship commonly termed the "Five Pillars of Islam" that provide the framework for the Muslim's spiritual life. The observance of these duties is regulated by individual conscience, and consequently, in real life, a spectrum of practice exists among Muslims.

The Five Pillars of Islam

Arabic Name	Meaning...
Shahadah	Declaring belief in the One God and His prophets, culminating with the final prophet, Muhammad, and intending to abide by the principles of Islam.
Salah	Worshipping God the Creator five times throughout the day as a way of maintaining God-consciousness and piety.
Zakah	Paying a special "purification" tax annually, if eligible, out of one's wealth to help the poor and needy.
Sawm	Fasting daily during the Islamic month of Ramadan as a spiritual exercise.
Hajj	Making a pilgrimage to Makkah once in one's lifetime to commemorate the trials of Prophet Abraham and his family in their efforts to reestablish monotheism.

1. SHAHADAH – DECLARATION OF FAITH

Why is the Shahadah important?

The *shahadah* represents the first pillar of Islam, upon which everything else is based. The *shahadah* is a two-fold declaration or statement—it is a denial of the worthiness for worship of anything except God, and an affirmation of Muhammad's prophethood (and thereby the prophethood of all previous prophets, since Muhammad is considered the last). The *shahadah* states: *"I bear witness that there is no deity except Allah (God), and that Muhammad is His Servant and Messenger."*

Making the declaration in sincerity formally brings a person into the fold of Islam. Other than repeating the *shahadah* in the presence of at least two Muslim witnesses, no particular ceremony (such as a baptism) is involved.

The *shahadah*, being the central theme of Islam, is repeated in the *adhan* (call to worship) and in the *salah* (formal worship) numerous times throughout each day. This practice serves to remind Muslims of their commitment to God and effort to live righteously.

2. SALAH – FORMAL WORSHIP

What is Salah?

Salah (or *salat*), the second pillar of Islam, is formal ritual worship. Muslims are required to perform the formal worship five times daily—at dawn, mid-day, in the afternoon, after sunset, and at night. *Salah* is an act which demonstrates that a Muslim's *shahadah* is not simply lip service, for a symbolic submission to God can be discerned in the various movements of the worship. Moreover, *salah* reinforces God-consciousness, reducing the likelihood of a Muslim's disobeying God and committing sins, and provides an opportunity to thank God for His blessings and to ask for His forgiveness. *Salah* also provides a respite from the day's challenges and cimcumstances, enabling a believer to refresh his or her intimate, personal relationship with God. Typically, after completing the formal worship, Muslims engage in *du'a*, or personal supplication, in which they sit quietly and thank God for His blessings and pray for good health, prosperity, happiness, assistance in times of distress, or anything one may desire. While *salah* is performed in Arabic, *du'as* may be said in any language.

The Daily Worship

Name	Typically Performed...
Fajr	early dawn, prior to sunrise
Dhuhr	shortly after mid-day
Asr	mid-afternoon to early evening
Maghrib	immediately after sunset
Isha	night-time, after dusk has ended

As implied above, the timings for the formal worship are determined by the movement of the sun in the course of the day. When the time for *salah* has arrived, a designated person called the *mueddhin* calls believers to assemble for worship. The call to prayer, performed in Arabic by the *mueddhin*, is called the *adhan*. Upon hearing the *adhan*, Muslims in the vicinity congregate at the nearest *masjid* (mosque). In most Muslim countries, the *adhan* can be heard some distance from the *masjid*, since *mueddhins* often make the call to prayer from the tops of minarets or use loudspeakers. Muslims who do not live near a masjid often use a daily worship time table to determine the times for prayer. Such time tables are prepared in advance using astronomical data.

What does salah involve?

Salah is a particular ritual of movement and prayers designed to demonstrate to God a human's self-understanding of his or her role as a created being. *Salah* is the foremost act of worship. Since *salah* involves various standing, bowing and prostrating positions, there are no pews or chairs in a *masjid*, the Muslim house of worship. Rather, the worship area is typically a simple, carpeted open space oriented towards the city of Makkah, where the *Ka'bah* is located. The length of time required to perform the *salah* depends on the number of *ra'kah*, or "units" of worship involved. For example, the early morning worship involves two units, the evening worship three units, and the other worship times four units. Each unit consists of standing, bowing, and prostrating (touching the forehead to the ground) twice. During each of the stages or positions, various verses from the *Qur'an* and supplications are recited in Arabic. In the case of congregational worship, an *imam* (leader) is chosen to lead the worshippers, who form rows behind him. The Friday noon worship is the main weekly worship when Muslims are required to pray in larger congregations.

The commonly used term "mosque" is a French word for Muslims' place of worship. For the sake of accuracy and self-definition, Muslims prefer the more correct Arabic word *masjid*, which means "place of prostration."

Adhan – The Call to Worship

Arabic Phrase	Meaning...
Allahu Akbar! Allahu Akbar! Allahu Akbar! Allahu Akbar!	God is Greatest! God is Greatest! God is Greatest! God is Greatest!
Ash-hadu-an La Ilaha ila Allah! Ash-hadu-an La Ilaha ila Allah!	I bear witness that there is no deity but the One God! I bear witness that there is no deity but the One God!
Ash-hadu An-na Muhammad-an Rasul-Allah! Ash-hadu An-na Muhammad-an Rasul-Allah!	I bear witness that Muhammad is the Messenger of God! I bear witness that Muhammad is the Messenger of God!
Haya Alas-Salah! Haya Alas-Salah!	Come to worship! Come to worship!
Haya Alal-Falah! Haya Alal-Falah!	Come to success! Come to success!
Allahu Akbar! Allahu Akbar!	God is Greatest! God is Greatest!
La Ilaha ila Allah!	There is no deity but the One God!

While praying in a *masjid* with fellow Muslims is recommended, usually Muslims worship wherever they may be—at work, at school, even at Disneyland, since a *hadith* states: *"The whole earth is a masjid."* The only requirement for a location used for worship is that it must be clean, dignified and that it provides sufficient space for the worship movements.

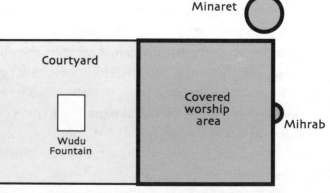

Major features of a Masjid

Muslims, regardless of where they live in the world, face towards the *Ka'bah* in Makkah during the formal worship. The *Ka'bah*, built by Abraham and his elder son Ishmael, is considered to be the first house of worship dedicated to the One God, and therefore serves as a spiritual focal point for Muslims. Contrary to one misconception, Muslims do not worship the *Ka'bah* while performing the *salah*. Simply, Muslims face *towards* the building as an act of unity, demonstrating a worldwide connection between all members of the *ummah* (Muslim community). Interestingly, since sunrise and sunset (and thus the worship times) move across the face of the earth, there is never a moment when someone isn't praying toward the *Ka'bah*.

No special attire is required of Muslims for performance of formal prayer, since Muslims are expected to offer the worship as part of their daily schedule, taking into consideration their professional environment or other situational factors. The only conditions for clothing are that they be clean and conform to standards of modesty.

What is said in the Muslim formal worship?

Muslims begin the *salah* by facing Makkah, and then raising their hands to their ears and proclaiming "*Allahu Akbar*" ("God is Greatest"). Worshippers proceed with a variety of movements and statements. An important component is the recitation of verses from the *Qur'an* during the standing position of the worship act. Worshippers may recite any verses from the *Qur'an* which they choose, following recitation of *Al-Fatihah*, the opening chapter of the scripture. This particular chapter is recited in each of the five daily worship times, since it embodies the core of the Islamic message. Due to its significance, it is also often recited to begin special programs, gatherings, or events.

Surah al-Fatihah (The Opening)

"Praise be to God, the Cherisher and Sustainer of the Worlds
Most Gracious, Most Merciful
Master of the Day of Judgement
Thee do we worship, and thine aid we seek
Show us the straight way,
The way of those on whom Thou hast bestowed Thy Mercy
Of those who do not earn Thine anger, nor go astray." (Qur'an, 1:1-7)

Muslims recite verses from the *Qur'an* by memory during prayer. These verses address themes and concepts that Muslims should ponder and learn from. Some themes include God's majesty, God's infinite wisdom and love for mankind, reward and punishment, justice and equality, among others.

Although it may sound like singing to some, the recitation of verses from the *Qur'an* is not subject to arbitrary intonations by individual reciters or worship leaders; in fact, reciters adhere to formalized principles and methods for reciting. Oral recitation of the *Qur'an* helps Muslims concentrate on the meaning of the words. Moreover, the beauty of the recitation often soothes and inspires believers.

3. SAWM – FASTING

What is Sawm?

The *Qur'an* enjoins Muslims to fast as a means of demonstrating commitment to God in the face of temptation and difficulty. *Sawm*, fasting for a period ranging from dawn to sunset, teaches Muslims self-restraint, patience, endurance, and obedience to God. Moreover, it puts into perspective the plight of those unable to obtain regular nourishing meals. When fasting, Muslims often discover a calm, inner peace which helps them become even closer to God.

In physical terms, fasting means not eating any foods, drinking any beverages (including water), or engaging in marital sexual relations from dawn to sunset. On the spiritual and moral level, it means struggling to develop self-restraint, God-consciousness and piety. Muslim strive in this month to curb all detrimental desires and negative or uncharitable thoughts, and to nurture love, patience, unselfishness and social consciousness.

> *"O you who believe! Fasting is prescribed to you, as it was prescribed to those before you, that you may learn self-restraint."* (Qur'an, 2:183)

When do Muslims fast?

Ramadan is the ninth month of the Islamic lunar calendar. It is a sacred month for Muslims because the first verses of the *Qur'an* were revealed to Muhammad in *Ramadan* 610 C.E. The *Qur'an* instructs Muslims to fast from dawn to sunset during *Ramadan*. Conscientious Muslims often fast a given number of additional days throughout the year in emulation of Prophet Muhammad, for the sake of enhancing personal piety. Muslims may also fast to atone for lapses in spiritual devotion.

Since *sawm* can be physically demanding, those who are unable to fast, such as pregnant or nursing women, elderly people, sick or injured individuals, are exempt. In place of fasting, these Muslims must make up missed fasting days at a later date. If this is not possible, they must instead arrange for the feeding of two persons for each day of fasting missed.

What does fasting entail?

During *Ramadan*, the entire family arises early in the morning (before dawn) to have a meal called *suhoor*. A variety of traditional and regional foods are prepared to nourish Muslims before beginning the day's fast. After the meal, Muslims offer the early-dawn *salah* (Fajr) and may read a while from the *Qur'an* before returning to sleep or preparing for the day ahead. During the day, the occasional hunger pangs and bouts of thirst remind Muslims of God and His bounty, which are often taken for granted. When sunset arrives, Muslims break the fast by having the *Iftar* meal.

In keeping with the tradition of Prophet Muhammad, Muslims break the fast with dates and other fruits and appetizers, and then offer the evening worship. Some time later, Muslims have dinner, usually in the company of extended family and friends.

After the night worship is offered, Muslims offer a special form of formal worship called *Tarawih*. Each night of *Ramadan*, Muslims perform up to twenty units of the *tarawih salah*, during which about one-thirtieth of the *Qur'an* is recited. In the course of the month, this enables the entirety of the *Qur'an* (over 6,000 verses) to be heard by believers joined in worship, reinforcing the message contained therein.

4. ZAKAH – MANDATORY ALMSGIVING TAX

What is Zakah?

Zakah (or *zakat*) is an act of worship in which eligible Muslims pay a specified amount of money (about 2.5% of one's accumulated wealth) as a tax to be used to

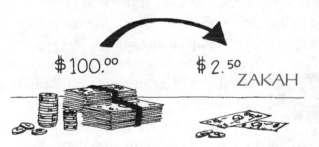

assist poor and needy persons in society. The annual payment of *zakah* "purifies" one's income and wealth by reminding Muslims that their possessions are in reality a trust and a test from God, to be used not only for personal benefit, but for the benefit of others as well.

In the present era, no centralized authority collects *zakah* funds. Rather, *zakah* monies are collected by local *masjids* and institutions throughout the world. According to Islamic Law, these monies may not be used for *masjid* administration, to pay salaries of general institutional staff, or for other items covered in a general budget. *Zakah* funds may only be used for distribution to several categories of legitimate recipients (homeless, orphans, etc.) and for the administrative apparatus that makes this service possible.

What is the purpose of Zakah?

Zakah helps to establish economic justice, by maintaining a minimal standard of living for the least fortunate members of society. Furthermore, for those with sufficient wealth to qualify, paying the *zakah* is a means of earning spiritual reward from God and divine reimbursement in the Hereafter. Conversely, neglecting to pay *zakah* is a grievous sin.

5. HAJJ – PILGRIMAGE TO MAKKAH

Muslims are required to perform the *Hajj*, or pilgrimage to Makkah at least once in their lifetime if they are physically and financially able to do so. *Hajj* is a time of turning away from the world in order to turn towards God and sincerely seek His forgiveness for past sins and errors. The rites of the *Hajj* commemorate the trials and sacrifices of Prophet Abraham, his wife Hajar, and their son, Prophet Ishmael. The city of Makkah, in modern-day Saudi Arabia, is the site of the pilgrimage because the *Ka'bah*, which was built by Abraham and Ishmael as the first "house of worship" dedicated to the One God, is located there. The *Hajj* takes place over several days in the early part of the twelfth month in the Islamic calendar, called *Dhul-Hijjah*.

Who must perform the Hajj?

Every year, over two million Muslims from all over the world, comprising the largest annual international gathering on earth, perform the *Hajj* rites. Being one of the pillars of Islam, the *Hajj* is required of every Muslim who is financially capable and whose health permits making the journey. Those without sufficient finances need not feel forsaken, since according to the *Qur'an*, God does not burden a person beyond his or her ability. Other acts of piety and worship ensure favorable

judgement on the Last Day for such persons. A Muslim whose physical condition may not permit travel and performance of the *Hajj* rites instead may pay the way for another to do so, thereby earning a similar reward.

Upon approaching the holy land, pilgrims enter a state of consecration (solemn dedication) known as *ihram*, and don the *ihram* attire, comprised of several sheets of white, unstitched, seamless cloth. Donning the *ihram* symbolizes a Muslim's leaving behind of the material world for the sake of God, and also reminds him or her of human mortality, since the white cloth evokes the image of the death shroud Muslims use to wrap the deceased. The collective sea of white created by millions of pilgrims also serves to reinforce Islam's egalitarian and universal ethos, reminding Muslims that all people are created as spiritual equals, and that only faith in God and righteousness in this life differentiates one from another.

What is the Ka'bah?

The *Ka'bah* is an empty cube-shaped brick structure measuring about forty feet per side, located in the city of Makkah, in modern-day Saudi Arabia. Interestingly, the English word "cube" comes from *Ka'bah*. Muslims believe the *Kab'ah* to be the original House of God on earth, rebuilt over the ages as a reminder of humankind's original monotheistic orientation. The foundation of the present structure was constructed by Prophets Abraham and Ishmael over four thousand years ago, in an age steeped in polytheism.

By the time of Prophet Muhammad, polytheism had once again reasserted itself and the tribes of Arabia had transformed the House of God into a repository for over three hundred tribal and regional idols and deities. After achieving success in proclaiming the message of Islam and gaining control of Makkah in 630 C.E., the Prophet removed all of the idols, rededicating the *Ka'bah* as a place for the worship of the One God.

Over the centuries, the *Masjid al-Haram* (sacred *masjid*) structure surrounding the *Ka'bah* has been renovated and expanded to accommodate increasing numbers of Muslim pilgrims and visitors. The *Ka'bah*, made of large bricks, has remained virtually unchanged. In order to preserve the structure and adorn it, the *Ka'bah* is covered by a black cloth, replaced annually, containing various phrases and verses from the *Qur'an* embroidered in gold and white thread.

Housed in one corner of the *Ka'bah*'s foundation is the Black Stone. This stone is believed to be a meteor sent from the Heavens as a sign to Abraham of God's pleasure and blessings. While constructing the *Ka'bah*, Abraham placed this token of God's affection into the developing structure. Many pilgrims touch or kiss the Black Stone during their circumambulations around the *Ka'bah*, though doing so is not required, nor does it serve any particular religious purpose. Contrary to one misconception, the Black Stone is not an idol or a representation of Allah.

THE MUSLIM SOCIETY

THE SHARI'AH – ISLAMIC LAW

What are the sources of religious authority in Islam?

There are two basic sources of authority in Islam. The first is the Speech of God embodied in the *Qur'an*. The second source of authority is the *Sunnah*, the words and deeds of Prophet Muhammad.

Shi'ah Muslims have a third authority for religion beside the above two authorities recognized by all Muslims. The teachings and writings of a number of early charismatic leaders called *Imams* descended from the Prophet's son-in-law Ali are an additional source for Shi'ahs, since they believe these descendants are infallible and consider their words and explanations nearly as authoritative as the *Qur'an* and *Sunnah*.

Muslim scholars use these sources in order to understand the principles of *Shari'ah* (Islamic Law) contained in them, and to develop legal opinions on existent as well as novel situations. The authentic sources also serve as criteria for differentiating between religiously-based actions or opinions and those resulting from other factors, such as culture, social status or circumstance. For example, some women in Muslim societies wear veils covering the face, yet to do so is not a requirement of the *Shari'ah*. In fact, Islamic Law requires that women cover all parts of the body *except* the hands, face and feet. The practice of veiling the face, therefore, cannot be attributed to Islam (though Muslim women may do it out of a sense of religiosity). Indeed many have surmised that such practice was adopted by Muslims after exposure to Byzantine Christian society, in which upper-class women wore face veils and remained secluded from the public.

What is Shari'ah?

The term *Shari'ah* is an Arabic word which means "the path" or literally "the way to a watering place." *Shari'ah* is commonly used to mean divinely-revealed "Islamic Law," which plays a central role in the lives of Muslims throughout the world. *Fiqh* is an Arabic term referring to the body of scholarship and jurisprudence developed over the centuries to interpret and implement the *Shari'ah*. Scholars recognize four main sources for developing *Shari'ah* and applying it to human situations: the *Qur'an*, the *Sunnah*, *Ijma* (consensus among Muslim scholars and jurists), and *Qiyas* (making deductions by analogy or precedent).

How was Shari'ah developed?

Within a hundred years of Prophet Muhammad's death, there began a great intellectual and scholarly movement among Muslims. The process of collecting, verifying, and codifying the *hadith* (sayings) of Prophet Muhammad had developed into a science of its own. Teachers and students of the *Qur'an* had begun writing *tafsirs*, or commentaries in order to explain the meanings of its verses.

In this era of conscientious effort and study, four schools (among many) of *fiqh*, or Islamic jurisprudence, rose to prominence. These schools, while all using the same sources for deducing laws and making judgments, varied in their interpretations on different issues. Due to varying social structures, cultures, and lifestyles of Muslims worldwide, these four schools gained popularity to different degrees in different parts of the world. A fifth school of jurisprudence (*Jafari*) arose among Shi'ah Muslims, providing legal guidance for Muslims in Iran, Pakistan, Lebanon and other places with significant populations of Shi'ahs.

Schools of Islamic Law		
Name	**Founder**	**Commonly followed in...**
Hanafi	Abu Hanifah (d. 767)	Turkey, Egypt, Pakistan, India, Afghanistan, Jordan, Syria
Hanbali	Ahmad ibn Hanbal (d. 855)	Iraq, Saudi Arabia, Gulf countries
Jafari	Jafar as-Saadiq (d. 765)	Iran, Pakistan, Afghanistan, Lebanon, Gulf countries
Maliki	Malik ibn Anas (d. 795)	North African countries, Bahrain
Shafi'i	Muhammad ash-Shafi (d. 820)	East Africa, Yemen, Central Asia, Southeast Asia, Jordan, Syria, Iraq

What is the role of Shari'ah today?

In terms of personal practice and fulfillment of religious obligations, Muslims around the world continue to look to these schools for guidance on issues of a legal nature. Muslim scholars continue to use principles of *fiqh* to deduce new approaches to life in the modern world that remain authentic to the injunctions of the *Qur'an* and *Sunnah*.

On a societal level, in some Muslim countries *Shari'ah* is implemented as the basis for the judicial system and for regulating the collective affairs of citizens. Other countries implement a hybrid of *Shari'ah* and civil law, first developed in these countries when colonized by European nations, while some others do not implement *Shari'ah* at all.

Muslims living as minorities in countries such as the United States abide by the civil laws of the land. However, because of the importance of *Shari'ah* in enabling the practice of Islam as a complete way of life, Muslims may express a desire for implementation of *Shari'ah* for themselves. Interestingly, in England, Muslims have established a religious parliament that works with the British government to enable implementation of Muslim personal laws, which deal with matters of marriage, divorce, inheritance, and other issues.

LEADERSHIP AND RELATED ISSUES

Is there a priesthood or clergy in Islam?

The use of the terms "priesthood" or "clergy" to describe Muslim religious leaders is inappropriate. In Islam, religious leaders or scholars are not ordained persons, nor do they belong to any kind of leadership hierarchy. Rather, they are simply individual Muslims who have acquired more religious knowledge than the average believer. Universities and specialized academies around the world, mainly in Muslim countries, provide relevant curricula for those interested in the various religious fields.

Different terms are used to refer to different types of scholars or leaders. An *alim* is one who has studied the *Qur'an*, *hadith*, and other texts extensively. A *faqih* is one qualified to make judgments based on the *Shari'ah*. A *hafiz* is one who has memorized the entirety of the *Qur'an*, while a *qari* specializes in reciting the *Qur'an* in a formal melodic manner. The term *shaykh* is an honorific title applied to respected learned men, elders or leaders, and in Sufism it takes on an added meaning: a *shaykh* is viewed as a spiritual master or guide for other believers. The term *imam* among Sunni Muslims designates a leader of the five daily prayers, and is used generically to refer to any religious leader who teaches courses, offers sermons, officiates marriages, and performs other duties. Within the Shi'ah tradition, the term *Ayatollah* (lit. "sign of God") is used as an honorific title for highly learned and pious religious authorities, and *Imam* designates a person with supreme religious authority.

While such persons play valuable religious and social roles within the community, it is important to note that they do not in any way serve as spiritual *intercessors* between individual Muslims and God.

What do the terms "Sunni" and "Shi'ah" mean?

At the time of Prophet Muhammad, the terms "Sunni" and "Shi'ah" did not exist — they developed later in Muslim history. After the Prophet passed away, Muslims were left to determine who should rightfully succeed him as the political leader (*khalifah*) of the Muslim community. Many were of the belief that a leader could be selected among any of the righteous and pious Muslims who demonstrated leadership abilities, and accepted the historical sequence of leaders comprised of Abu Bakr, Umar, Uthman, and Ali, followed by dynastic leaders such as the Umayyads, Abbasids and others. This has come to be known as the majority viewpoint, designated "Sunni" in reference to these Muslims' reliance on the *Qur'an* and *Sunnah* of Muhammad as the sources of religious doctrine and practice.

Others believed that the position of khalifah had been initially conferred by the Prophet upon his cousin and son-in-law Ali ibn Abu Talib. In the ensuing years, this difference of opinion was perpetuated, as the *Shi'ah* ("supporters" or "partisans" of Ali) continued to hold that authority belonged to Ali and his descendants. The Shi'ah supported various descendants of Ali as rightful leaders in opposition to the effective rulers of the time, and succeeded in ruling certain regions at certain times.

In the largest branch of Shi'ism, Ali and eleven successive descendants are given the title *Imam* by Shi'ahs and they are considered the rightful, designated successors of Prophet Muhammad. The Arabic term "imam" literally means "leader" or "model," and is commonly used to refer to the leader of formal congregational worship. Shi'ah Muslims use the term more reverentially, since the Imams are believed to be sinless and to have knowledge of things unknown to others. Furthermore, the teachings of the Imams are given weight similar to that of the *Qur'an* and *Sunnah* as a source for correct belief and practice.

Shi'ahs also believe that the twelfth and final Imam (born 868 C.E.) continues to live in a miraculous state of occultation (concealment from human view). The Hidden Imam is believed to enact God's plan in the world and provide continued guidance on behalf of the first Imam Ali.

What is Sufism?

Sufism is a branch of Islam that deals with the purification and perfection of character towards the ultimate aim of love and closeness to God. Prophet Muhammad, when asked about the perfection of character replied, "It is to worship God as if one sees Him and if one does not see Him, to know that He sees you." Sufism is rooted within the body of Islamic revelations and tradition. Just as the Muslim must purify the external self in preparation for worship, so, too, must the believer strive to reach a state of inner of purity in worship and approach his Lord.

Through the practice of Sufism, a Muslim may learn to purify the self of all vices such as envy, anger, deceit, pride, arrogance, love of praise, greed, stinginess, and disregard of the poor and needy. Sufism teaches one to adorn oneself with the perfect attributes of tolerance, discipline, contentment, repentance, forgiveness, compassion, loving kindness, sincerity, self-restraint, piety, reliance on and remembrance of God, watchfulness and many, many others. A famous Muslim scholar of the 14th century, Ibn Taymiya, describes the Sufi as follows: "The Sufi is a person who purifies the self from anything which distracts from the remembrance of God."

The history of Islam is replete with the phenomenal influence of Sufis and Sufism on all aspects of life: spiritual, intellectual, artistic, and political. Some of the most prominent figures in literature, such as Rumi, Jami, Saadi, and Attar, were Sufis. The spread of Islam throughout Africa, Central Asia, the Indian sub-continent, Malaysia and the Far East was accomplished through the work of many great Sufi saints. In the nineteenth century, the resistance to Russian imperialist expansion into Chechnya and Daghestan was conducted successfully for forty years by Sufis under the leadership of Shaykh Shamil. The sultans of the Ottoman Empire all had Sufi advisors. Even the organization of the Franciscan monastic order was patterned on the rules of a Sufi order with whom St. Francis had been in contact in the Holy Land. The list of examples is really endless.

Are there saints in Islam?

Saintly personages have played an important role in the history of Islam, though the concept of a "saint" in Islam is different than in Catholicism. Every religious tradition finds its most perfect expression in the life and teachings of its founder and early companions and then in those who came later who most perfectly embody the message and its way of life. Indeed the most perfect flowering of Islam can be seen in the lives of its "saints." Prophet Muhammad is the pattern and perfection of all saintly qualities. Following him in rank are his companions and their successors, and pious people in later generations, who while not perfect, attain a high degree of God-consciousness, moral behavior, wisdom, and kindness.

Though fewer in number with each passing generation, saints continued to arise and exert their influence throughout the course of Islamic history up to and including the present day. According to tradition, in each century a particularly pious individual renews and revives the religion of Islam, to rid it of any accretions or deviations that are the inevitable consequences of human fallibility. These saints have been men and women of vast learning, impeccable character, and selfless devotion. On a popular level, the love of saints and the seeking of their guidance and prayers has long been a part of the Muslim life. Indeed the injunction of the Prophet to "seek knowledge even unto China" has been understood in part as an order to seek the guidance of the rightly-guided wherever they may be.

What does Islam say about representations of holy figures?

Muslims have avoided making pictures or representations of any of the prophets, or even the Companions of Prophet Muhammad, lest the revered person represented visually becomes an object of worship. Muslims, in general, are extremely wary of any practices which might lead to ascribing divinity to anyone or anything as a partner to God. Bearing this in mind, however, Muslims have been ordered in the *Qur'an* to recite the praises of, and send blessings upon, Prophet Muhammad as the servant of God. Further, Muslims have generally considered artistic representations of God's creations to be a form of either pride or foolish disrespect. Thus, traditional Muslim artists and artisans generally avoided realistic depictions of known figures, and instead developed very beautiful geometric styles of artistic expressions, especially in all forms of architectural crafts like ceramics, woodwork, and stone masonry as well as carpet weaving and calligraphy, to name but a few. Traditional books on zoology and biology and other materials contained stylized depictions for educational purposes.

MARKING TIME

What kind of calendar do Muslims use?

The *Hijrah* (migration of Prophet Muhammad from Makkah to Madinah in 622 C.E.), marks the starting point of the Islamic calendar, comprised of twelve lunar months. Each lunar month begins when the new moon's crescent becomes visible every 29 or 30 days. Muslims use such a *Hijri* calendar for various religious obligations such as fasting during *Ramadan*, celebrating the two *Eid* holidays, and performing the *Hajj*.

The Islamic Lunar Calendar

Name of Month	Meaning...
Muharram	"The sacred month."
Safar	"The month which is void."
Rabi al-Awwal	"The first spring."
Rabi ath-Thani	"The second spring."
Jumada al-Awwal	"The first month of dryness."
Jumada ath-Thani	"The second month of dryness."
Rajab	"The revered month."
Shaban	"The month of division."
Ramadan	"The month of great heat."
Shawwal	"The month of hunting."
Dhul Qadah	"The month of rest."
Dhul Hijjah	"The month of pilgrimage."

Since the lunar year is about eleven days shorter than the solar year, dates in the Islamic calendar "move back" eleven days earlier every year in relation to the commonly-used Gregorian calendar. Consequently, over a period of about thirty-six years, the events in the Islamic calendar cycle through the various seasons. In this way, Islamic events do not acquire specific seasonal connotations, and Muslims around the world have the opportunity to experience these events under varying environmental conditions. The names of the months were used in Arabia even before the advent of Islam, and may have first been employed on a solar calendar.

What does the crescent and star symbolize?

Often Islam is associated with a symbol of the crescent moon and a star. This symbolism may be related to the fact that the lunar calendar plays a significant role in Islam. Some historical sources posit that the symbol was appropriated from the Byzantines when Muslim forces defeated them in the late seventh century. In any case, the crescent and star icon does not constitute an official symbol in Islam, though it adorns many countries' flags, currency, masjids and other structures.

What is the holy day of Muslims?

Muslims' special day is Friday. On this day, the mid-day formal worship is replaced by a special congregational worship called *Salat al-Jum'ah* (Friday prayer). This worship is preceded by the *khutbah*, a short weekly address given by the *imam* (worship leader). After the worship is completed, Muslims often enjoy lunch with each other and socialize. In Muslim countries, many Muslims do not work on the day of *Jum'ah*. Despite its importance as a day of congregation, *Jum'ah* is not a "sabbath" day, since Muslims are not obliged to observe a "day of rest" for fear of punishment.

Muslims attend their local *masjids* on other days as well. On weekends, many *masjids* or Islamic Centers hold classes or events designed to teach young Muslim children or new Muslims about their faith. Special guest speakers are often invited to address the community, and various meetings and conferences are held.

What are some important dates in the Islamic year?

There are a number of important dates in the Islamic calendar. Some of them are described below:

The first day of the month of *Muharram* announces the new *Hijri* year, and the tenth of this month is known as *Ashurah*. Muslims believe the tenth of *Muharram* to be the day when Moses led his people out of Egyptian bondage. It is also the date on which the Prophet's grandson Husayn and his family were killed by the forces of Yazid, the second Umayyad ruler, who, it is believed, usurped rightful leadership of the Muslim community from Husayn. All Muslims, but especially Shi'ahs, mourn this tragic event.

Laylat al-Qadr, or the "Night of Power," is one of the last ten nights of the month of *Ramadan*. It is significant as the night on which, in 610 C.E., Prophet Muhammad received the first revelations of the *Qur'an*. Muslims commemorate this night, believed to fall on the 27th of *Ramadan*, by offering additional prayers and supplications late into the night. It is said the blessings of praying on this night are greater than those received by praying for a thousand months.

The 27th of the month of *Rajab* is the date for *Laylal al-Miraj*. On this date Muslims recall Prophet Muhammad's miraculous journey from Makkah to Jerusalem and thence to Heaven atop the heavenly steed known as *Buraq*. According to tradition, during this Night Journey and Ascension, which took place in 619 C.E., Muhammad received instructions for instituting the *salah*, or formal worship. Islam's connection with previous monotheistic religious traditions was also reiterated, as the Prophet met all of his predecessors during his experience, and led the prophets in prayer at place of the Masjid al-Aqsa in Jerusalem.

What holidays do Muslims celebrate?

There are two major holidays in Islam:

Eid al-Fitr takes place on the first of Shawwal, the tenth month of the Islamic lunar year, after the end of Ramadan, the month of fasting. The holiday celebration begins early in the morning with a special congregational worship. The *Eid* prayers are often held in a specially designated gathering place, such as a park or convention center, meant to accomodate large numbers of Muslims from several local *masjids*.

After the prayer, the *imam* (worship leader) delivers a short *khutbah* (sermon or address). Then everyone rises to their feet to greet and hug one another. The rest of the festival's observances are held among family and friends, and include visits, shared meals, new clothes, gifts for young children, and lots of sweets. In Muslim countries, festivities are often in evidence for three or more days. In order to share the spirit of the occasion with all members of society, Muslims pay a special nominal charity tax which is used to purchase food, clothing and gifts for needy persons.

Eid al-Adha takes place on the tenth of *Dhul Hijjah* (the twelfth month of the Islamic lunar calendar), after the majority of *Hajj* rituals are completed by pilgrims. Around the world, Muslims share in the spirit of the *Hajj* by observing the *Eid* festivities in their own localities. The day's observances are similar to those of *Eid al-Fitr*, with the addition of a special sacrifice—Muslims commemorate Prophet Abraham's willingness to sacrifice his elder son Ishmael when God commanded him to do so as a test of his commitment. Since God miraculously provided a lamb to Abraham which took the place of his son, Muslims recall the event by sacrificing animals such as lambs, goats, sheep, cows or camels. The sacrifice may be performed any time after the *Eid* morning prayers until the evening of the twelfth of *Dhul-Hijjah*. The meat of the sacrificed animals is distributed to the poor or needy, and portions are kept for one's own family and friends during this time of extra charity and hospitality.

Do Muslims celebrate the birthday of Prophet Muhammad?

The birth of Prophet Muhammad is commemorated with the festivities of the *Mawlid an-Nabi* (Prophet's Birthday) on the twelfth of the month of *Rabi al-Awwal*. Most Muslims take the opportunity to study more about the Prophet and his deeds, since Muslims consider him to be the best example of how one should lead his or her life. While the Prophet's birth date is an important event recognized by Muslims, it is not an official religious holiday like *Eid al-Fitr* or *Eid al-Adha*.

GENDER AND FAMILY ISSUES

What does Islam say about the equality of men and women?

According to Islam, men and women are spiritually equal beings created from a common origin. All of the religious obligations in Islam are incumbent upon both women and men, such as daily worship, fasting, performing the *Hajj*, etc. God's mercy and forgiveness apply equally to men and women. The following *Qur'anic* verse, arguably the first gender-equity statement in any major scripture, illustrates this point:

> *"For Muslim men and Muslim women,*
> *For believing men and believing women,*
> *For devout men and devout women,*
> *For true men and true women,*
> *For men and women who are patient and constant,*
> *For men and women who humble themselves,*
> *For men and women who give in charity,*
> *For men and women who fast,*
> *For men and women who guard their chastity,*
> *And for men and women who engage much in God's praise,*
> *For them has God prepared forgiveness and great reward."*
> (*Qur'an*, 33:35)

As a consequence of physiological, psychological and other distinguishing factors embodied in men and women by the Creator, the rights, responsibilities, and roles of men and women are believed to naturally differ. Muslims believe that God has assigned the responsibility of providing financially for the family to men, and the important responsibility of fostering a God-conscious and righteous family to women. Such roles do not preclude women from having careers and earning income or men from helping to raise a family. Rather they provide a general framework for Muslim society, designed to reinforce the concept of a nuclear family unit.

The guidelines for men and women's roles are also meant to ensure dignified and proper relations between people of the opposite sex. Minimal mixing of the sexes in Muslim societies should not be construed to imply inequality or confinement. Rather, such measures are designed to protect individuals from unsolicited attention, inappropriate sexual attraction, adultery and fornication, and possibly even forms of violence such as rape.

What are the rights of women in Islam?

In the seventh century, a revolution in women's rights occurred due to the message of the *Qur'an* and its directives for forging a just and righteous society. In pre-Islamic Arabia as in other places in the world, women were considered little more than chattel, with no independent rights of their own. The *Qur'an* specifies the natural and inherent rights of women as well as men, and enjoins people to act in line with God's teachings of justice and equity. Some of the rights of women elaborated in the *Qur'an* and *Sunnah* include the right to own and inherit property, the right to obtain an education, the right to contract marriage and seek divorce, the right to retain one's family name upon marriage, the right to vote and express opinions on societal affairs, and the right to be supported financially by male relatives (husband, father, brother, etc.).

Such rights were unheard of in the seventh century, yet were implemented to varying degrees in Muslim civilization throughout the last fourteen hundred years. It is also important to recognize that only in the last two centuries have such rights been available to women in Western societies. Clearly, common stereotypes regarding women's rights must be carefully considered, and the current practice of Muslims in various countries and regions must be examined within the context of history and with in light of the sources of Islam in order to ascertain the degree to which Muslim women are able to exercise their rights today. Prevailing cultural factors must also be taken into account.

How do Muslims view marriage and divorce?

Marriage is highly encouraged in Islam, as families are seen as the cornerstone of Muslim society. Men and women are enjoined by the *Qur'an* and the guidance of Prophet Muhammad to live with mutual love, respect, and affection. For example, a well-known *hadith* instructs Muslim men that *"the best among you is he who is kindest to his wife."*

In Islam, marriage is a relationship based upon a legal contract agreed upon by the persons getting married. The marriage ceremony itself is very simple. A religious scholar, *imam* or learned person within the community performs the ceremony in the presence of at least two Muslim witnesses. After the bride and groom have signed the marriage contract and a gift for the bride has been agreed upon, the couple may state their vows in front of family and friends. Often, at weddings, the *imam* gives a short marriage sermon as well. After the marriage bond has been declared, it is customary for the groom and his family to host a *walimah* (marriage feast) for friends, relatives, and community members.

Divorce is highly discouraged in Islam. While permissible, it is viewed as a last resort after stages of time for reevaluation have passed and all attempts at reconciliation have been made. Both men and women can seek divorce in Islam, and contrary to one popular misconception, men may not instantaneously pronounce a divorce by stating "I divorce thee" three times. After a divorce, a woman must wait for a period of three months, called *iddah*, before remarrying, in order to ensure that she is not pregnant by her previous husband. While modern DNA technology may render such a practice obsolete by identifying the father of a newly conceived child, the *iddah* serves the additional purpose of maintaining the dignity of women and the sanctity of marriage.

Are arranged marriages an Islamic tradition?

Islam requires that both the prospective bride and groom must consent to marry each other. Islam does not condone the compelling of individuals to marry. In this sense, arranged marriages are not an Islamic practice. However, in many Muslim cultures, marriages often result when a prospective bride and groom are introduced to each other through relatives or mutual friends, though nothing precludes two eligible people who know each other to decide to marry. Typically, the man and woman are given an opportunity to talk with each other in a family setting and gauge their compatibility. If the prospective bride and groom agree to the match, the two families jointly make wedding preparations. These types of "introduced" marriages are more "Islamic" than traditional arranged marriages. Though not an Islamic requirement, some families formalize the bond through an engagement ceremony if the wedding is planned for some future moment.

There is no specific age after puberty at which either men or women must be married. Much depends on factors such as schooling, career, and other life circumstances. However, because marriage is seen as a solidifying force in a Muslim society, Muslims who reach eligible age (typically from early to mid-twenties) are encouraged to get married. Beyond the individual benefit of finding a life-companion, marriage is seen as a protection from illicit sexual behavior. The Prophet Muhammad described marriage as "fulfillment of half of the faith."

"Among His signs is this, that He created for you mates from among yourselves, that you may dwell in tranquility with them, and He has put love and mercy between your hearts. Verily in that are signs for people who reflect." (Qur'an, 30:21)

"Women are garments (protective clothing) for men and men are garments for women." (Qur'an, 2:187)

How do Muslims view dating and mixing of the sexes?

Dating as it is commonly understood in western society is not permitted in Islam. For Muslims, physical interaction, an almost inevitable component of dating, is only permissible within the bonds of marriage. While Muslims often find themselves in mixed environments in Western society, and may participate in certain coeducational group activities, as a general rule they observe a degree of self-segregation.

Naturally, the proper and productive functioning of society requires the talents and contributions of all its citizens, male and female. Therefore, Islam provides guidelines for etiquette and behavior in order to enable full participation of men and women while at the same time fostering righteous societies. Some guidelines pertain to appropriate forms of interaction between the genders, while others pertain to kinds of clothing men and women should wear in the interest of modesty. By observing such guidelines, women and men are able to interact productively in society, minimizing potential for sexual harassment, uninvited attention, disrespect, or acts of violence fostered by provocative dress or conduct.

How are birth and childhood viewed in Islam?

In accordance with tradition, soon after birth the father of the child whispers the *adhan* (call to prayer) in the right ear of the newborn. This act signifies that the child has been born into a community centered around worship of the Creator.

Also in accordance with tradition, many Muslims perform a ritual known as *aqiqah* for newborns. The birth-hair of the newborn is shaved off to signify a new phase of life outside the womb. The *aqiqah* is usually performed on the seventh day after birth, though it may be done later. In addition, a goat or lamb is typically sacrificed for a feast of thanksgiving. During the feast, family and friends pray that God blesses the child with good health, happiness, and protects her or him from all physical harm and evil influences.

After birth or in early childhood, male children are circumcised in accordance with the *Sunnah*. The circumcision may be seen as a symbolic act, performed in homage to the great sacrifices to which Prophet Abraham and his son were committed. Circumcision may also reiterate Muslims' view of Islam as a continual message unfolded through history, since the practice is found among Jews, descendants of the followers of the earlier prophet Moses. Circumcision is not obligatory upon adult converts, since it is not a strict requirement of *Shari'ah*.

In certain regions of the world, female circumcision is a cultural tradition, practiced by a small number of Christians, Muslims and tribal animists. Such practices violate the integrity of human beings and are contrary to the most basic teachings of Islam, and find no sanction in Islamic Law.

As for education, the *Qur'an* repeatedly reminds readers that "those who know" are not the same as "those who know not," and a *hadith* of Prophet Muhammad states that seeking knowledge is an obligation for both men and women. Consequently, most Muslim parents tend to be very involved in their children's education. Teachers are highly respected and are seen as allies in cultivating knowledge and in presenting positive role models for students. It is not uncommon to find Muslim parents helping their children learn their lessons, encouraging them to excel, and rewarding them for good grades. Even when children are performing well in their studies, many Muslim parents want to meet with teachers, and if their child is not performing up to standards, parents usually side with educators in trying to encourage students to improve.

Naturally, religious education is very important to Muslims. At an early age, children begin memorizing the short verses of the *Qur'an*, especially *al-Fatihah*, the opening chapter. In some Muslim cultures, around the age of four, a *Bismillah* ceremony is held to signify a child's readiness to begin learning to read the *Qur'an* in Arabic. This tradition, while not a part of the *Sunnah*, is very common among Muslims of the Indian subcontinent (Pakistan, India, Bangladesh, Sri Lanka), Southeast Asia (Indonesia, Malaysia) and Central Asia. Some time later, when the child has completed his or her first full reading of the entire *Qur'an*, an *Ameen* ceremony is held. The *Ameen*, like the *Bismillah* event, is not a religious obligation and is a tradition among some Muslims meant to celebrate a child's reading of the *Qur'an*.

LIFE AND DEATH

What is Islam's view on reproductive issues?

Naturally, the course one's life takes is affected by the choices one has and the options one may exercise. Consequently, Muslim scholars have provided a number of responses to various long-standing and contemporary reproductive issues to help Muslims make responsible and appropriate life decisions.

Islam encourages Muslims to have children, yet teaches that parents must plan wisely and responsibly to ensure children have a decent standard of living devoid of undue hardship. Thus, Islam permits birth control, so long as both the mother and father are aware of its use, and so long as the forms used are reversible and/or temporary. Condoms, diaphragms, intra-uterine devices, and the pill may be used, in contrast to tubal ligation or vasectomy, which in most cases would not be acceptable. Medical means of birth control that do not prevent conception but rather affect a fertilized ovum are not acceptable as well. The so-called "morning-after" or "abortion pill" falls into this category.

According to the majority of scholars, abortion is not permitted in Islam, except when a mother's life might be at risk if she were to continue her pregnancy, in which case the actual life of the mother takes precedence over the potential life of the unborn child. In the absence of such complication, the fetus represents potential life from the moment of conception, and therefore its right to life under the *Shari'ah* must be protected. Islam's views can be attributed to several *Qur'anic* verses, including: *"Do not slay your children because of poverty — We will provide for you and for them."* (6:151). In Muslim societies, the government has a responsibility to assist low-income families, thereby minimizing the perceived need for abortions.

Surrogate parenting involves a woman bearing the child of another woman unable to do so. This practice is not an option for Muslims, since the child of a couple is carried by another individual outside the framework of a marriage contract between a man and woman. The ultimate emotional and social ramifications for the individuals as well as society at large are considered too great for surrogacy to be acceptable in Muslim societies. Women unable to bear children are rewarded by God for exhibiting patience and forebearance in this life, and have the hope of fulfilling their most profound wishes in what is considered the real, eternal life of the Hereafter.

Fertilization with the sperm of a non-husband is a grievous crime and sin under the *Shari'ah*. Reproduction is only legitimate within the confines of the marriage bond, involving the genetic material of the married individuals.

How does Islam view homosexuality?

The *Qur'an* forbids homosexuality:

> *"Of all the creatures in the world, will you approach males and abandon those whom God created for you as mates?"* (26:165).

By analogy, the above verse applies equally to females. While Muslims may condemn acts of homosexuality, the *Shari'ah* requires that the basic rights of life and safety of all human beings must be protected. Thus, Muslims may not accost or treat proclaimed homosexuals unjustly.

What does Islam say about suicide and euthanasia?

According to Islam, all life is sacred. Deliberate and calculated suicide is considered a total lack of faith in God. To kill oneself is just as forbidden as to commit murder, and is a sign of ungratitude towards God. Muslims believe that God tests people in this life, yet does not burden a soul beyond what it can bear. To perservere in times of distress and to call upon God for comfort and strength is an important element in the Muslim lifestyle and worldview. Ultimately, Muslims are to call upon God's infinite Mercy and seek an appropriate solution to life's dilemmas.

> *"And most certainly shall We try by means of danger, and hunger, and loss of worldly goods, of lives and of (labour's) fruits. But give glad tidings unto those who are patient in adversity."* (Qur'an, 2:155).

Euthanasia, the practice of terminating someone's life to end their perceived suffering, is not permissible in Islam (cases where the physical body is being kept alive through artificial means are another matter). Muslims believe that all things are ultimately according to God's decree, and pain and suffering must be dealt with through prayer and repentence. Moreover, only God determines the time and manner of one's death, and to "preempt" God is seen as a rejection of God's divine Wisdom and plan. Muslims also believe that the suffering of righteous believers in this life will be compensated by immeasureable happiness and reward in the Afterlife.

How do Muslims deal with death?

Muslims believe that life and death are in God's hands, and that God appoints a time for each person to pass from this existence into the next. Muslims are reminded regularly that death is inevitable and that the actions of this life determine one's status in the Hereafter. When a person dies, his or her relatives are urged to be patient and accepting of God's decree. It is permissible to cry and express grief at the death of a loved one, though excessive lamentation is discouraged. Though grieving may never fully end, the period of outward mourning typically lasts no more than three days.

> *"Every human being is bound to taste death; and We test you (all)*
> *through the bad and the good (things of life) by way of trial: and unto*
> *Us you all must return."* (Qur'an, 21:35).

As soon as possible after death, the body of the deceased person is washed and wrapped in plain white linen and placed in a simple wooden coffin (if one is necessary). The body is then taken to the cemetery, where it may be carried by community members on a bier to the gravesite. Before burial, a special congregational worship service is offered, and prayers are made for God's mercy upon the deceased. For Muslims, burial represents human beings' return to the most elemental state, since we were fashioned from earth by the Creator. Thus cremation, preservation of the body, internment in above-ground mausoleums, or other methods are not allowed in Islam.

The affairs of the deceased may be handled via a will or testament. The *Qur'an* prescribes specific means for disbursing inheritance to spouses, children and relatives. Many scholars have indicated that organ donation is permissible in Islam, and is considered a profound charitable act.

When a married man dies, his wife must not remarry until at least four months and ten days have passed. This period of waiting, known as *iddah*, allows her to determine whether she may be pregnant with her deceased husband's child, which would affect issues of inheritance, lineage, and related matters. Even in an age of sophisticated DNA technology, in which the identity of parents can be ascertained quite accurately, the waiting period serves to honor the deceased husband and preserve the dignity of the marriage bond.

DAILY LIFE

What is the Islamic concept of worship?

The regular performance of acts of worship, such as *salah* (formal worship) and *sawm* (fasting), is essential for acknowledging God's authority in one's life and for spiritual growth. While these acts involve specific practices and statements, Islam does not teach blind, ritualistic imitation. Muslims believe that God does not want from His servants absent-minded movement of the tongue and body—rather, He wants attention of the heart and sincere actions. Consequently, the *neeyah*, or intention that one has before fulfilling a particular obligation, counts a great deal. Indeed, a hadith states: *"Actions are judged according to their intentions."*

Interestingly, the Arabic word *ibadah* means "worship" as well as "service." Thus, to worship God means not only to love and exalt Him but also to serve Him by living in accord with His guidance in every aspect of life, to enjoin goodness among people and forbid wrong-doing and oppression, to practice charity and justice, and to serve Him by serving humanity.

> *"It is not righteousness that you turn your faces toward East or West; but it is righteousness to believe in God and the Last Day and the Angels and the Scripture and the Messengers; to spend of your wealth, out of love for him, for your kin, for orphans, for the needy, for the wayfarer, and for those who ask, and for freeing slaves; to observe prayer and give charity; to fulfill the contracts that you have made, to be firm and patient in pain and in adversity, and time of stress: such are those who are sincere. Such are the God-conscious."* (Qur'an, 2:177)

What dietary regulations must Muslims observe?

A general rule of *Shari'ah* is that anything that is not expressly *haram* (forbidden) or that doesn't lead to *haram* acts is considered *halal* (permissible). This principle applies to foods as well. In the *Qur'an*, very few items are expressly forbidden, namely the flesh of swine, blood, meat of carcasses, meat of predatory animals, and meat of animals slaughtered in the name of anything other than the One God. When Muslims slaughter animals for consumption, they pronounce the name of God during the act, symbolizing recognition of His bounty and His role as Creator of all things. Such blessed meat is termed *halal*, a designation similar to "kosher" used by Jews. In fact, the *Qur'an* states that meat from the *Ahl al-Kitab*, or "People of the Book" (Christians and Jews) is permissible for Muslims to eat. Such legal provisions serve to reiterate the common monotheistic bond of the three Abrahamic religions. At the same time, many Muslims do not eat meat from commercial sources, since rules for slaughtering animals in Islam differ from those current in America.

Aside from certain foods, substances which are detrimental to human health or livelihood are also prohibited. Chief among these is alcohol, since it alters one's mental state and impairs one's abilities for reasoning and judgement, affects one's moral compass, and interferes with the proper functioning of the biological senses. Along these lines, and considering their powerful addictive qualities, so-called recreational drugs such as cocaine, heroine, and marijuana are prohibited in Islam as well. The societal ramifications of alcohol and drug abuse in terms of automobile accidents, conflict and divorce, and crime and violence are well-documented, affirming for Muslims Islam's wisdom regarding even casual use of such substances.

Mild stimulants such as caffeine found in chocolate, coffee, tea and soft drinks do not have direly adverse effects, and therefore such foods and drinks are permissible, so long as one does not feel addicted to them. Some scholars view smoking as *haram*, due to its addictive nature and clearly detrimental effects upon a person's health and well-being.

What is the dress code for Muslims?

The *Qur'an*, *Sunnah* and the consensus of Muslim scholars provide a general Islamic dress code that applies to both men and women. In practice, Muslim peoples have integrated the Islamic dress code with their own local cultures, customs and geographical conditions, resulting in great varieties of Muslim dress from region to region.

From the Islamic perspective, clothes are meant for cover and simple adornment, not for demonstration of social status or attraction of the opposite sex. In other words, guidelines for dress are meant to prevent men and women from being objects of desire and temptation. Islamic dress is based on a few guidelines: clothes should be loose fitting, such that the shape of the body is not highlighted; clothes should not be transparent or sheer; clothes should cover certain prescribed parts of the body—for men, minimally the body from the navel to the knee (though it is extremely rare to see a male in a Muslim setting who isn't covered from ankle to neck), and for women, everything except for face, hands and feet. Muslim women who cover according to these guidelines are said to be in *hijab*. The term is also used commonly to describe the head covering or scarf worn by many Muslim women. A Muslim woman who covers her hair does so out of a sense of religious obligation, piety and modesty, and to be clearly recognized as a Muslim woman.

As indicated above, the dress code is interpreted according to cultural setting. In Muslim countries, people often dress in traditional attire. Men may be seen wearing a long tunic-like garment (*thawb* or *jelabiyah*) that extends to the feet, or a shorter shirt-like garment that extends below the hips. Many Muslim men also wear a religious or cultural cap or head dress, such as a *kefiyah*, *kufi* or *fez*. The traditional Muslim woman's dress varies greatly from culture to culture: the full-length chador is popular in the Gulf states and Iran, long coat-like garments are typical of Syria and Jordan, colorful long dresses and turbans can be seen in West Africa, and wrapped saris are common in India. It is also not uncommon in some Muslim countries to see Muslim men and women wearing Western styles. In the United States, immigrant Muslims can be seen in varying traditional clothing, whereas native-born or second and third generation Muslim men and women typically wear Western styles of clothing adapted to the Islamic requirements of covering.

Considering the greater degree of covering required of women, due to pronounced physical differences between men and women, men have a particular responsibility to avert their eyes and treat women with dignity and respect.

> *"Tell the believing men to lower their gaze and to be mindful of their chastity: this will be most conducive to their purity- verily, God is aware of all that we do. And tell the believing women to lower their gaze and to be mindful of their chastity, and not to display their charms (in public) beyond what may (decently) be apparent thereof; let them draw their head-coverings over their bosoms."* (Qur'an, 24:30-31)

CONTEMPORARY ISSUES

What is the "Nation of Islam"?

The Nation of Islam was founded in the 1930s by Elijah Poole, who later became widely known as Elijah Muhammad. The organization was formed to address the civil rights concerns of African-Americans in the United States, and advocated complete segregation from "white" society. In order to rally the support of African-Americans seeking an alternative to traditional approaches to long-standing injustices, the Nation used terminology borrowed from the religion of Islam, and simultaneously developed an elaborate mythology to support its claims of black racial superiority.

After the death of Elijah Muhammad in 1975, his son Warith Deen Muhammad renounced the race-based teachings of the Nation. He and his followers then joined the mainstream community of Muslims. The Nation was later revived by Louis Farrakhan. Today, according to a study by Numan and Associates (Washington D.C.) there are less than 10,000 followers of Farrakhan.

Because the Nation holds that Elijah Muhammad was a prophet of God and that his mentor W.D. Fard was God Incarnate, the Nation cannot be considered a branch or subset of Islam by mainstream Muslims. Such beliefs are contrary to the basic doctrines and tenets of Islam as defined in the *Qur'an* and *Sunnah*. Furthermore, the race-based orientation of the Nation contradicts the universalist outlook advocated by worldwide Islam.

Who are "Black Muslims?"

The term "Black Muslim" has been used to describe a follower of the Nation of Islam, though it is considered a confusing misnomer by mainstream Muslims, since Islam is practiced by people of every race and ethnicity. For Muslims the term "Black Muslim" is no more valid than "White Muslim." So-called "Black Muslims" are not to be confused with Muslims (followers of universal Islam) of African-American or African origin.

Who was Malcolm X?

Malcolm X (born Malcolm Little in 1925), was a very energetic and controversial spokesperson for the Nation of Islam during the 1960s. After becoming disillusioned with the organization and its leader Elijah Muhammad, Malcolm X renounced affiliation with the group and set about to clarify his knowledge of Islam as practiced worldwide. He traveled to Makkah, Saudi Arabia to perform the *Hajj*, the journey that all Muslims aspire to make at least once in their lives. Upon his return, he took the name El Hajj Malik El Shabazz, and began developing a new organization to further the cause of African-Americans in the U.S. without the racial trappings of the Nation. Malcolm began telling audiences about his remarkable experiences in the holy land and transformation from someone who believed in the superiority of blacks to someone who believed in the universal equality of all human beings irrespective of race, a cornerstone of mainstream Islam.

Malcolm X was assassinated on February 21, 1964 while making an address at the Audubon Ballroom in New York City. Unfortunately, his death occurred before his new-found ideas and views gained currency and attention, leaving him with an unwarranted stigma among segments of American society because many have remained fixated on his previous nationalist orientation.

How do Muslims view people of other faiths?

Because Muslims accept that Jesus and the Biblical prophets were indeed true Prophets of God, Muslims identify a great deal with teachings found in Christianity and Judaism. Most scholars of religion agree that Judaism, Christianity and Islam share a common monotheistic heritage and world view. The similarities between the three faiths are in many ways greater than the differences. In recognition of this, some scholars call the three religions the "Abrahamic" faiths, since all three trace their history back to the patriarch Abraham.

While cherishing the similarities, Islam holds that by the time of Prophet Muhammad, Rabbinic Judaism and the Christian Church had forgotten, misinterpreted and modified the original teachings of the ancient prophets, including Abraham, Moses, David and Jesus. Muslims believe that within Judaism monotheism had been compromised with the raising of the opinions and interpretations of rabbis to the same level of authority as God's word. In addition the concept of a chosen race or group of people is seen as a misapplication of God's ancient covenant with Abraham, since God promised to bless all of his progeny. For Muslims, righteousness is the only criterion for a special relationship to God. Within the Christian Church, monotheism was compromised by raising Jesus to the level of God and making him part of the Trinity. Consequently, God selected another prophet to complete the prophetic teachings and reestablish the purity of the primordial monotheistic faith centered solely around worship of the One God.

Despite these criticisms of Judaism and Christianity, Islam advocates positive relations and designates Christians and Jews as *Ahl al-Kitab*, or "People of the Book," recognizing the divinely revealed origin of the two faith traditions. Historically, Muslims accepted Jews and Christians as *dhimmis*, or protected communities within the Islamic state, allowing them complete freedom to practice their religion and enforce their own religious laws. Moreover, the *Shari'ah* states that injuring non-Muslims, damaging their religious sites or otherwise violating their rights as citizens of the state are strictly forbidden. This protected status was conferred on Hindus, Buddhists and Zoroastrians as well in the course of history. Today, principles of *Shari'ah* remain in effect regarding harmonious and constructive relations between Muslims and people of other faiths.

What is Jihad?

The Arabic word *jihad* means "struggle" or "exertion" and refers to any spiritual, moral or physical struggle. Upon returning from a battle, the Prophet Muhammad is reported to have said, *"We are returning from the lesser jihad to the greater jihad—jihad against the self."* For Muslims, *jihad* means struggle in the cause of God, which can take many forms. In the personal sphere, efforts such as obtaining an education, trying to quit smoking, or controlling one's temper are forms of *jihad*.

Jihad as a military action is justified in two cases: struggle to defend oneself, or others, from aggression and struggle for freedom of religion and justice. The *Qur'an* says *"Tumult and oppression are worse than killing"* (2:217), and therefore must be thwarted. Human beings as responsible agents of God on earth are compelled to exert themselves to protect the oppressed and strive to create righteous societies.

Systematic, forced conversion to Islam is a historical myth. Muslims defeated hostile forces (Byzantines and Persians for example) and gained control of new lands where Islamic rule was established, yet non-Muslim inhabitants were not forced to become Muslims. Islam clearly condemns such actions: *"There is no compulsion in religion."* (*Qur'an*, 2:256) For various reasons, and in the course of time, many non-Muslims did find the message of Islam appealing, however, and converted to Islam, resulting ultimately in the transformation of society at all levels.

Because *jihad* is a highly nuanced concept, and because the term stems from an Arabic root meaning "struggle," the term "holy war" is an inappropriate rendering or definition.

Does Islam promote violence and terrorism?

Contrary to popular misconception, Islam does not condone terrorism. Prophet Muhammad and the Rightly-guided *Khalifahs* (caliphs) prohibited the killing of civilians and non-combatants in the course of warfare. The *Qur'an* says, *"Fight for the sake of God those that fight against you, but do not attack them first. God does not love the aggressors."* (2:190) Moreover, the *Qur'an* indicates that taking one life unjustly is like taking the life of all humanity, providing a strong moral deterrent to indiscriminate bloodshed. Besides prohibiting the killing of non-combatants, the *Qur'an* and the Prophet also prohibited the torturing of prisoners and the senseless destruction of crops, animals and property.

Struggle against injustice is a key, distinctive concept in Islam. Through the ages, the concept of righteous struggle has inspired Muslim peoples and movements to stand up against oppression and tyranny, as in the case of the wars of independence against colonialism. African-Americans, in recent decades, have been drawn to Islam, in part, because of its activist stance.

While some Muslim extremists may perpetrate acts of terrorism, this does not diminish the legitimacy of righteous struggle against oppression and injustice experienced by Muslims in many parts of the world (often at the hands of so-called Muslim leaders). Indeed, such persons actually violate the teachings of Islam.

> *"O you who have attained to faith! Be ever steadfast in your devotion to God, bearing witness to the truth in all equity; and never let hatred of anyone lead you into the sin of deviating from justice. Be just: this is the closest to being God-conscious. And remain conscious of God: verily, God is aware of all that you do." (Qur'an, 5:8).*

In any case, there can be no such thing as "Islamic terrorism," despite the fact that such terms have become a popular oxymoron. The adjective "Islamic" cannot be applied to what some misguided Muslims do. See the section on *Teaching with Sensitivity* for more on inappropriate usage of various terms.

What is "Islamic Fundamentalism"?

Historically, the term "fundamentalist" was originally applied to those Christians who took the Bible as literal scripture, as opposed to allegorical truth, among other implications. Muslims, on the other hand, have always considered the *Qur'an* to be the literal Speech of God. Moreover, there are no degrees of belief regarding the basic doctrines of faith.

Nowadays, the term "fundamentalist" is used to describe any adherent of the major world religions who holds that faith is a model for modern life and plays a role in political, economic or social matters. Furthermore, in terms of Islam, it is often applied to those Muslims, better termed "extremists" who use unjustified means to achieve particular political goals. A further problem is that the term is often wantonly and pejoratively used in the media to describe Muslims who base their views and actions on a particularly religious worldview. In such cases, sincere, practicing Muslims who perform the daily worship, avoid alcohol, or wear *hijab* are labelled inappropriately, even though their behavior may be normative.

Thus, "Islamic Fundamentalism" is a confusing misnomer, resulting in broad generalizations and misunderstanding.

What is Islam's view on human rights and social justice?

According to Islam, human beings are the noblest creations of God, endowed with consciousness and freedom of choice. The *Qur'an* states that God has made human beings His trustees or stewards on the earth. Muslims see this world as God's field, and human beings as the farmers and caretakers. Muslims believe humanity's ultimate task is to build a world that reflects the will of God. Thus, Islam is balanced in its concern for salvation in the Hereafter as well as peace and justice in the present world. Islam places great emphasis on social justice for all people. Muslims consider it an obligation to oppose all who exploit, oppress, discriminate, and deal unjustly with people.

> *"O you who believe, be upholders of justice, witnesses for God even if it be against yourselves."* (*Qur'an*, 4:135)

Muslims understand the goal of Islam to be the spiritual upliftment of the individual and productive development of society. The ultimate consequence of rejecting God and His guidance is a selfish, pleasure-seeking, corrupt, and unjust society. Conversely, the natural consequence of obedience to God's laws and living according to His guidance is a society of peace, equality, freedom from want, dignity for all, and justice.

As-salaam Alaykum — "Peace Be Unto You"
The Muslim Greeting, in Diwani Calligraphic Style

Teaching with Sensitivity

Teaching about religion can be tremendously challenging. Not only must educators take care to use accurate and balanced materials to supplement textbooks, they must also follow established ground rules for teaching about religion.

Additionally, educators are responsible for recognizing the increasingly diverse nature of the American classroom and understanding the needs of students from different ethnic, cultural, and religious backgrounds. Of course, parents also have a duty to inform their child's teachers about any special needs or considerations. This is especially true for Muslim parents, since Muslim children sometimes feel uncomfortable about bringing certain religious issues to the attention of their teachers. This reticence may, unfortunately, interfere with a Muslim student's ability to fulfill certain religious obligations.

Consequently, it would be tremendously helpful if educators became familiar with the particular needs of their Muslim students. By extension, this effort would serve to promote a climate of respect and understanding for all students in our diverse and pluralistic society.

A FEW WORDS ABOUT SENSITIVITY

MUSLIM BELIEFS AND PRACTICES

Islam, Judaism and Christianity share a common historical and theological bond with the patriarch Abraham. Consequently, Muslims share much in terms of history, values, and beliefs with Jews and Christians. Followers of Islam, Judaism and Christianity share a common belief in God, angels, prophets, holy scriptures, and a Day of Judgement. While important differences exist in how these basic components of belief are understood, there are nevertheless far more similarities among the three faith communities than many realize.

Differences are more pronounced in regards to various religious *practices* found in the three faiths. In addition, cultural norms prevalent in a given society may not conform fully to a lifestyle predicated upon Islamic teachings. To accommodate Muslim students' commitment to values and behavior inculcated by Islam, teachers are requested to respect their Muslim students' dedication to daily formal worship, fasting during *Ramadan*, and other religious obligations. Students who dress modestly, and particularly female students who wear a scarf or other head covering (commonly designated *hijab*) should be made to feel comfortable and respected.

PERCEPTIONS AND STEREOTYPES

Muslim students report that at times, they feel that they are treated differently from others by teachers as well as fellow students, due to lack of knowledge about Muslim beliefs and practices. Muslim students are sometimes taunted for not participating in certain student events such as dances, and Muslim girls are sometimes harassed for their manner of dress. During periods of tension in the global political arena, Islam is often maligned and Muslims may face unwarranted backlashes from fellow Americans. Some Muslim students, especially recent immigrants, speak with accents, leading others to view them as foreigners who do not really belong here. This animosity is reinforced by the notion propagated by some that Islam is "their" religion, not "ours." Such views are untenable considering that over six million Americans profess faith in Islam, and Muslims comprise one of the largest religious groups in the United States.

Muslims are also acutely aware of stereotypes and the miseducation that often results from their perpetuation. It may be useful for teachers to bring up common stereotypes about Muslims and then discuss them to explore their roots and determine why they are inaccurate or misleading. Of course, to accomplish this, educators must have a good understanding of the stereotypes, as well as a firm knowledge of Islamic beliefs and practices. Teachers must also be able to differentiate between religious and cultural practices, and distinguish the teachings of Islam from the actions of Muslims, as Muslims exhibit different levels of faith and practice. Furthermore, since no central religious authority exists in Islam, Muslims may differ in some of their interpretations of religious rules and obligations. Different Muslims will have different feelings and thoughts on specific issues. For example, some Muslim parents and students feel that making a pledge of allegiance to the American flag (or any national flag for that matter) is inappropriate, arguing that all allegiance is to God alone. Other Muslims see the pledge of allegiance as an indirect form of thanks to God for providing a land of liberty and opportunity in which to worship and prosper.

ACCURACY AND BALANCE

Naturally, teachers must exhibit impartiality and objectivity in their teaching style and approach. It is very important for educators to know the proper spellings, meanings, pronunciations and usages of vocabulary associated with Islam. For example, believers in Islam are collectively called "Muslims," not "Moslems," "Islamic people" or "Muhammadans." Furthermore, educators should be wary of terms and usages commonly found in print and broadcast media. For example, the word *jihad* is often defined by journalists as "holy war," despite the fact that its literal meaning is "effort" or "striving," and applies to many spheres of life. Another term commonly employed inaccurately in the media to describe Islamic renewal movements around the world is "fundamentalism."

Besides taking into consideration the above comments, teachers may want to ask parents about the value and accuracy of certain supplementary teaching materials, and solicit their input in selecting resources. On an administrative level, school districts might consider establishing some form of interfaith education committee to help define and develop a mutually acceptable format for teaching *about* religion in the classroom. Such a group should be comprised of open-minded, enthusiastic, and committed parents, teachers, and administrators striving to enhance sensitivity and balance in the classroom.

GROUND RULES FOR TEACHING ABOUT RELIGION

The study of world religions has been deemed essential for promoting global literacy, encouraging cross-cultural understanding, and giving depth to historical studies. Teaching about religion also provides an opportunity to explore ethics and value systems implemented by people around the world.

In recent years, educators have been grappling with standards for fair and accurate treatment of religions in instructional materials. These efforts have yielded what might be called a set of ground rules which may be applied to classroom teaching as well as instructional material content. For example, the Program in Humanities and Human Values at the University of North Carolina published *Ten Suggestions for Teaching About Religion*, and the Public Education Religion Studies Center (PERSC) at Wright State University developed *Criteria for Evaluating Curriculum Materials and Programs*. The salient points of these works, which are predicated on the concept that teaching must not violate the First Amendment of the Constitution as interpreted by the Supreme Court, are summarized below:

✦ Teaching about religion may be interdisciplinary as well as included within the social studies and humanities.

✦ The approach should include understanding from both within and outside the religious tradition studied and include both institutional and personal religious phenomena.

✦ Subject matter may legitimately include both the history and literature of the religion, as well as religious thought and the relation of religion and culture, distinguishing between historical facts and confessional facts.

✦ Material and methods should avoid reductionism (e.g. using only psychology or only sociology of the religion) and one-sidedness (i.e. they should present both the traditional and modern viewpoints, in addition to the contemporary relevance and meaning of the historical material).

✦ Methods of presentation should be open-ended, seeking not consensus but understanding and appreciation of the values that lead to different religious expressions, especially with the objective of breaking down stereotypes and of helping students to accept the internal validity of religious experiences other than their own.

Teachers are encouraged to review such ground rules from time to time and employ them in the classroom. Guidelines such as these should also serve as the basis for selecting instructional and resource materials.

PARENT - TEACHER - SCHOOL RELATIONS

Since Muslim parents place great emphasis at home on their child's education, teachers are encouraged to get parents involved in the affairs of their child's school. Considering the increasing number of Muslims in America, it would be useful for schools and districts to have Muslim parents involved in the PTA and other organizations to ensure that the needs of Muslim students are being met and that parents' concerns are being heard. On a side note, if parents from diverse backgrounds are invited to a meeting or function, the menu should reflect sensitivity towards the invitees. To accomodate Muslim, Buddhist, Hindu, or Jewish parents, for example, the following might be appropriate: a pot-luck can be arranged rather than a wine and cheese gathering; vegetarian entrees can be provided in addition to meat dishes; pork or ham dishes and products can be avoided or alternatives provided. Such efforts foster fuller participation by all members of the community.

In order to facilitate the enrollment and registration of new immigrant students, the school may suggest that parents get foreign documents, such as transcripts, immunization records, etc., translated into English. Muslim parents of diverse backgrounds in the community may be requested to assist in this process. It may also be useful to encourage Muslim parents in the area or district to form a committee which would designate a liaison with the school who could respond to various situations or concerns involving Muslim students, and who could serve on any shared decision-making councils regarding student affairs.

It's important for teachers and school officials to remember that many Muslim parents, for religious or cultural reasons, choose to wear traditional, ethnic attire. This preference should not prejudice a teacher in any way. Also keep in mind that every family is unique as a result of cultural, linguistic, ethnic, educational, occupational, and social factors. Bear in mind that religious sensibilities among Muslims vary as well. For example, some Muslims refrain from shaking hands with members of the opposite sex, while others do not. Do not feel personally offended if your offer to shake hands is politely declined. Other behavioral or cultural differences may be encountered, and teachers are encouraged to show patience and good-will.

CURRICULUM ISSUES

Some aspects of western education are viewed with reticence by Muslims, as they tend to undermine Islamic values and principles. For example, much of western art focuses on the human form, and nudes are a prominent component of paintings by renowned artists such as Gaugin, Renoir, and many others. The concept of modesty in Islam makes viewing such works a strange exercise for some Muslims, though doing so may seem quite ordinary for others. Moreover, the emphasis on the human form appears to reflect a human-centered view of the world, rather than the God-centered one found in Islam.

After the age of puberty, classes necessitating mixed dancing are not appropriate for Muslim students, whether cultural or other types of dances are involved. There are varying views among Muslims about single sex folk or cultural dancing for older children. Some Muslims also disapprove of music. It would be beneficial to provide Muslim students with an alternative activity if they desire not to participate for religious reasons.

Drama classes or exercises involving performance of scenes from the Nativity, or acting as deities, gods, or goddesses of mythology, may be objectionable to some Muslims. Other dramatic roles, classroom acts, and role plays are generally acceptable, as long as the issues discussed in this section regarding modest dress, mixing of the sexes, and physical contact are taken into consideration.

Regarding school outings, many Muslim parents are unlikely to allow mixed-sex outings over a weekend or longer period, though they probably would permit single-sex outings of similar nature. Day-long field-trips typically meet with no disapproval. Organizers of such events should keep in mind the needs of Muslim students, such as time for worship, *halal* (lawful) foods, privacy in showers and bathrooms, and appropriate forms of cross-gender interaction.

Further details, as well as concerns regarding Physical Education classes, are addressed under the subheading *Religious Needs of Muslim Students*.

LANGUAGE ISSUES

Transliteration of Arabic Terms

An important issue in discussing Islam is how to transliterate Arabic terms. Standardization is beginning to take place in academic circles. Because Arabic contains some sounds that do not correspond easily to Latin letters, a system of ellipses and symbols has been devised that is quite accurate, but not suitable for young students in a survey course. Consequently, many authors of materials on Islam use modified versions of the standard academic transliteration system. For example, Arabic vowel sounds are limited to "a," "i," "u," both long and short sounds, with "y" used both as a consonant and vowel, as in English.

Terms Related to Islam and Muslims	
Incorrect	Correct
Hejira	Hijrah
Kaaba	Ka'bah
Koran	Qur'an
Mecca	Makkah
Medina	Madinah
Mosque	Masjid
Moslem	Muslim
Muhammadan	Muslim
Muhammadanism	Islam
Shi'ite	Shi'ah

Thus, the transliteration "Muslim" is preferable to "Moslem" because it better enables the casual reader to reproduce the sound of the original word. Similarly, "shaykh" or "shaikh" better reproduces the original than "sheik." Writers, educators, and others should not be tempted to reproduce common mistransliterations (and thus, mispronunciations) under the guise of familiarity, as this clashes in the ears of Muslims, and does not contribute to a mutually respectful dialogue.

See the adjacent chart for commonly mistransliterated words along with corrections. Definitions of the above terms may be found in the *Quick Reference Glossary*.

Usage of Terms

ISLAM, ISLAMIC, AND MUSLIM

Another very common problem in materials related to Islam is incorrect or inconsistent use of terminology. Fortunately, the era when Islam was dubbed "Mohammedanism" as a parallel construct to Christianity and Buddhism has come to an end. Nowadays, the most frequent errors encountered relate to the use of the terms "Islam" or "Islamic" and "Muslim." An additional complication is that categories and terminology taken from Christian discourse and history are inaccurately used to describe very different categories and institutions in Islam.

Islam is the name of the religion whose final Prophet was Muhammad, and simply means a state of peace achieved through submission to God. *Muslim* is the name used for an adherent of the Islamic faith. Authors have created misunderstanding by confusing adjectival expressions concerning Islam. The term *Islamic* is accurately applied only to what pertains directly to the faith and its doctrines (such as Islamic law, Islamic worship, Islamic celebrations, Islamic values, principles and beliefs). The term Islam belongs to the realm of the aspiration, the ideal, the pure faith. We may acquire knowledge from this realm from authentic Islamic sources, and we may examine its constructs, interpret its doctrines and describe what is required of adherents of the Islamic faith; however, we may not describe a person or any historical phenomenon as Islamic.

To illustrate the problems inherent in usage, an author or educator might employ a seemingly benign formulation like "Islamic women" or "Islamic populations," even "Islamic countries," when "Muslim" women, populations or countries are clearly meant. When the historical phenomenon and cultural content begin to diverge from what is Islamic (doctrinally speaking), the situation becomes more problematic. Some scholars have tried to identify and describe phenomena such as an "Islamic city," "Islamic trade routes," "Islamic villages," as though the religion includes a blueprint for such cultural forms. At their worst, such incorrect adjectival constructions produce oxymorons such as "Islamic terrorists" and "Islamic militants" or "radical Islam" or "Islamic extremist groups," frequently used uncritically even while the same text states clearly that Islam is a religion of moderation, not radicalism, one that condones neither wanton violence nor extremism, much less terrorism, which is expressly forbidden by the most basic limitations placed upon legitimate warfare by Islamic doctrine.

The simplest solution is to use the terms "Islam" and "Islamic" solely for what pertains to the religion, and use Muslim as an adjective to denote the works and acts of Muslims, or groups of people and their institutions (such as Muslim women or men, Muslim population, Muslim countries or civilization, Muslim art, Muslim government or leaders, Muslim extremists). The important distinction is that human interpretation of Islam by Muslims is necessarily imperfect, and that persons, cultural artifacts and institutions are derived from and informed by Islamic precepts with admixture of secular, regional and ethnic influences. In short, human acts and constructs fall short of being purely Islamic, and therefore may not be denoted as such.

CHURCH, CLERGY AND CLERIC

The most commonly *borrowed* terms used in discussion of Islam are "Church" and "Clergy" or "Cleric." A basic level of accuracy requires explaining that Islam recognizes no central religious authority or institution of persons charged with authoritative interpretation of religion to believers. Yet treatments of Islam too often fall back on the use of the term "church" to mean an official institution of some sort, without defining any more closely what is meant.

Texts commonly refer to the lack of separation between "church and state" in the Islamic concept of government. In this instance, it is far more accurate to drop both terms, which were paired by historical events in Europe, referring instead to

the lack of separation between "the realm of religion and the realm of human political affairs." More simply, one might substitute "religion and government."

Muslims recognize no "church," "clergy" or "clerics" who act as intermediaries in the Muslim's relationship with God. The word "clergy" is often pressed into service to describe a Muslim scholar, prayer leader, or even a teacher of religious matter. This usage is extremely problematic. Firstly, the English, Christian term refers to an ordained person, used in opposition to the term "laity." Such a distinction does not exist in Islam. Second, the term "clergy" is too imprecise, since Muslim religious scholars play a wide variety of social roles. Thus, under the term "clergy," a variety of Muslim figures might be meant: an *alim* (scholar of religious knowledge), a *qadi* (judge), an *imam* (leader of prayer), or a *shaykh* (respected leader). Within the Shi'ah tradition, a *mujtahid* is a scholar qualified to make original decisions regarding the Islamic Law. These scholars and leaders often fulfill other economic and social roles as well. Common denotations and connotations of the word "clergy," in other words, have no resonance in Islam or Muslim society.

THEOCRACY

If one follows the incorrect description of the Muslim government as a theocracy, then the *khalifah* (successor to Prophet Muhammad) himself would also be a member of the "clergy." However, the type of government described by the term "theocracy" is an impossibility in Islam.

Theocracy is defined in *New Lexicon Webster's Dictionary* as: "government by priests or men who claim to know the will of God; a state thus governed." "Knowing the will of God" in the sense of governing implies not a general mandate based on an established body of scripture, but day-to-day divine rule subject to unpredictable change by authorities receiving orders from God. Government by prophets may be considered theocracy — one can argue that the rule of Moses, David, Solomon and Muhammad was theocratic, but rule by successors is no longer such. In the case of Islam, the *khalifahs* presided over states based upon the rule of law. The source of that law was two-fold: the *Qur'an* and *Sunnah*. However, scholars agree that the *khalifah* himself was not above the law — his mandate reached no farther than upholding established Islamic Law. Unlike a ruler who presides by divine right, for example, a Muslim ruler may be dismissed, reprimanded, criticized (as were all of the *khalifahs*) or act as the defendant in a court proceeding in a civil suit while in office. He may not abrogate the Law, but is subject to it. No aura of holiness attaches to him. No matter how much pomp became attached to Muslim rulers in history, or how remote they became from their subjects, they never acceded to the status of priests or god-kings. Thus, use of the terms "theocracy" or "theocratic" should be avoided in reference to Islam.

FUNDAMENTALISM AND FUNDAMENTALISTS

These terms have become so common in journalistic and scholarly usage that they have wandered deep into the conventional wisdom. This in itself is a phenomenon worthy of historical note. In world history courses, however, such terms should not be used uncritically. One would assume that the original meaning of the term will be studied in connection with Protestantism, and that mutations and applications of the term in various historical periods will be traced, before its contemporary usage is introduced. In this context, the term "fundamentalism" is a historic artifact used as modern parlance to describe a form of dedication to religious over secular life. Uncritical use is not permissible, particularly when it appears as a knee-jerk addition to the title of any Muslim, Jew, Christian or Hindu who holds that religion is more than a personal phenomenon. Its use as a synonym for "extremist," "fanatic," "radical" is equally unacceptable.

Historically, "fundamentalist" was originally applied to Christians, later referring to those Christians who took the Bible as literal as opposed to allegorical truth, among other implications. Nowadays, the term has expanded in meaning to include almost any adherent of the major world religions who still believes that faith is a model for modern life. Antipodal to "fundamentalist" is probably "secularist." A related pair of opposites is "modernist" versus "traditionalist." These terms carry considerable historical baggage of which students should be made aware before they can evaluate their applicability.

Several trends in the history of Christianity are relevant to the development of these complex ideas. The European struggle for a secular state took place in the context of two phenomena foreign to the Muslim world: an organized Church with worldly authority, and post-feudal, national monarchies legitimized by or heading a Church. Western scientific enterprise also developed its dichotomies between the spiritual and secular realms, between matter and spirit, and a sharp divide between tradition and modernity. This Christian historical environment is unlike either that which spawned Muslim science, or that of Chinese or Japanese science and technology. Western science developed in spite of and often in opposition to the Church and seldom in alliance with Biblical scholars, though some segments of the Christian community supported scientific inquiry. This situation was exacerbated where scientific influence entered Europe from the Muslim (so-called infidel) world. The Creationist debate in education is a contemporary illustration of this historical opposition. Western science, based of necessity on secular assumptions, gained momentum as it carried religious reinterpretation and capitulation in its wake. Religious revival in the West has often been an anti-modern sentiment. Scholars and popular commentators alike often assume this is the case with Islam, as well. Accepted uncritically, however, this view is an example of how Europeans assume that their own experience is universal. On the contrary, these notions have little resonance in Muslim thought and practice, whose scientific impulse existed in alliance with, or at least in an atmosphere of tolerance with Islam. Even where Greek philosophy caused temporary intellectual indigestion in Muslim scholarly and political circles, there was no Islamic "Church" hierarchy to bring sanctions against scientists. The pursuit of "secular" science was no maverick, dangerous endeavor in the Muslim world; it was patronized and encouraged at the highest levels long before the Renaissance or Western penetration.

Given the nature of the *Qur'an* and *Sunnah* and its relationship to Islam and Muslim practice, it is hard to transfer a notion of fundamentalism to the belief system. Since Islam enjoins obedience and submission to God's commands as stated in the *Qur'an* and exemplified by His prophets, there are no degrees of belief and practice in regards to the basic doctrines of faith. With regard to literal interpretation of scripture, the *Qur'an* itself states that some verses are to be understood allegorically, some are general principles and some are direct injunctions to be followed to the letter. The very nature of the *Qur'an* differs markedly from the Bible, and the two scriptures have a very different history.

A term, or category that better expresses the phenomenon that "fundamentalism" is intended to describe is religious renewal (*tajdid*) and resurgence. These terms are preferable to "revival." Many such historic and contemporary Muslim movements of renewal and resurgence labeled "fundamentalist" refer to models from among Muhammad's loyal companions, the "Rightly-Guided" *Khalifahs*, the Muslim equivalent of American "Founding Fathers" or "framers." Many of these Muslims in the modern world wish to renew their societies according to virtuous models, principles of good government and balanced social life based on the historic precedent set by those close to the source. Most adherents of these ideas are not anti-modern Luddites who want to return to nomadic life forms and archaic standards of living, any more than American admirers of the Founding Fathers prefer the horse over the jumbo jet.

The salient point is that fair, critical and informed use of terms promotes constructive and differentiated understanding of "the other." The term "fundamentalist" has pejorative overtones, causing people to dismiss a group of ideas, pigeon-hole or stereotype trends in thought before they have investigated their content.

Muslim Names

There are over 1.2 billion Muslims around the world with diverse languages, cultures, and ethnicities. Of these, about 15-18% are Arabs. However, because Arabic is the religious language of Islam, it plays a central role in the lives of all Muslims, irrespective of their particular native language, such as Urdu, Swahili, or English. As a consequence, great numbers of Muslims throughout the world have Arabic first names or surnames.

Generally, the names of Muslims have positive or sublime meanings, and may serve as a basis for developing one's identity and personality. One of the first important duties for Muslim parents is to select a meaningful name for a newborn child. Some parents name their children after important persons in Muslim history, such as the prophets, their companions and relatives, or successful leaders, scientists, or poets. Others choose a name reflecting the relationship between the human being and the Creator. These names often include an attribute of God, with the prefix *Abd* (servant) designating the named person, as in Abd al-Rahman, "servant of the Most Merciful." Still others choose names designating particular characteristics or implying beauty, patience or other traits. For example, Ameenah means "trustworthy" or "faithful" and Ahmad means "most praised."

Some Common Arabic Muslim Names

Girls' Names	Meaning	Boys' Names	Meaning
Ameenah	*Trustworthy*	Abd al-Baseer	*Servant of the All-Seeing*
Aqeelah	*Intelligent, Sensible*	Abd al-Majid	*Servant of the Glorious*
Asma	*Eminent*	Amjad	*More Glorious*
Basimah	*Smiling*	Anwar	*More Radiant*
Deebah	*Golden*	Faysal	*Decisive*
Farah	*Joy, Cheerfulness*	Habeeb	*Beloved*
Haleemah	*Gentle*	Hakeem	*Ruler, Sovereign*
Hibah	*Gift, Present*	Hasan	*Handsome, Good*
Jameelah	*Beautiful*	Ibrahim	*Abraham*
Kareemah	*Noble, Generous*	Iqbal	*Responsiveness*
Khadeejah	*Precocious*	Jamal	*Beauty, Grace*
Layla	*Night*	Khalid	*Glorious, Eternal*
Maymunah	*Fortunate, Blessed*	Lateef	*Refined, Gentle*
Najmah	*Star*	Masood	*Happy*
Rasheedah	*Pious, Conscious*	Mustafa	*Chosen*
Sakeenah	*Tranquility*	Nabeel	*Noble, Generous*
Salmah	*Peaceful*	Ridwan	*Goodwill, Pleasure*
Sameerah	*Jovial, Lively*	Saleem	*Secure, Safe*
Tasneem	*Fountain of Paradise*	Shakir	*Thankful*
Uzma	*Greatest*	Siraj	*Heavenly Lamp*

Having an Arabic name, however, is not required of Muslims; nor is it a prerequisite for one who decides to embrace Islam. Indeed, many Muslims have non-Arabic names, such as Elizabeth (English), Jeffrey (English), Jean (French), Shabnam (Persian), and Serpil (Turkish). At the same time, many new Muslims do take on Arabic names as an outward symbol of their newly established spiritual worldview and identity. Teachers should also be aware that many Muslim women retain their maiden names after marriage, invoking a right established by Islamic Law over 1400 years ago. Consequently, teachers may encounter situations in which a student's last name differs from that of his or her mother, without any specific con-notations, such as divorce.

The adjacent chart provides a list of some common Muslim names and their meanings. Teachers can use these names for student assignments or activities related to Islam and Muslims. Due to variations in transliteration, different spellings for these names may be encountered in the real world; the spellings in the chart have been chosen for the sake of making pronunciation easier. It is important for teachers to ask students with non-Western names how their names are pronounced in order to learn them, rather than encouraging students to go by nicknames selected from the English language. Many Muslims are especially sensitive to this, since the right to an honorable, designated name is seen as a basic human right in Islam.

RELIGIOUS NEEDS OF MUSLIM STUDENTS

In Islam, one becomes accountable for fulfilling religious obligations at the age of puberty, although many Muslim children often learn and perform the various duties at an earlier age. Muslim students in public schools may express a desire to adhere to certain religious principles or fulfill certain religious requirements. A number of relevant issues and needs are discussed below:

Salah (Daily Worship)

Muslims perform the formal worship or prayers known as *salah* five times daily. At least one of these worship times falls during the typical school hours, and thus some suitable arrangement should be made for students who wish to fulfill this obligation. With adequate safety precautions in mind, teachers should provide Muslim students who are conscientious about observing their prayers with a private corner or empty classroom for a few minutes during lunch-time or afternoon recess for this purpose. Keep in mind that since women are exempt from performing the formal worship during menstruation, Muslim teenage girls who typically pray at school may be reluctant to explain why they're suddenly changing their behavior, and you may assume that this is the reason if the change is temporary.

Jum'ah (Friday Congregational Worship)

For Muslims, Friday is a day of congregational worship. *Salat al-Jum'ah* (Friday prayer) is preceeded by an address or sermon by the *imam* (leader of worship), and takes the place of the mid-day worship (*Dhur*) performed on other days. The congregational worship service typically requires 30 to 45 minutes, and falls close to most students' lunch hour. Some Muslim students may wish to make arrangements to leave campus temporarily to attend congregational prayers at a local *masjid*, while others may request the use of an empty classroom to conduct the worship service themselves.

Dietary Guidelines

The *Qur'an* specifies which foods are lawful and unlawful for Muslims to eat. Regarding meat, Islam prescribes a particular method for slaughtering lawful animals for consumption, designed to minimize suffering for the animal. The meat of lawful animals such as cows, goats, chickens, among others, slaughtered in this prescribed manner is commonly designated *halal*, or lawful.

The *Qur'an* states that the food of Jews and Christians is lawful for Muslims, provided that certain conditions of method, cleanliness and purity have been fulfilled. Some Muslims eat meat of lawful animals available commercially in American society, while others, believing the above-mentioned conditions have not been met, eat only meat which has been slaughtered in the prescribed way by a Muslim butcher.

The meat of swine is prohibited in Islam. Muslims do not eat pork or foodstuffs made with pork derivatives such as gelatin and lard, and certain enzymes. Examples of such foods include pepperoni pizza, non-beef hot dogs, and certain brands of refried beans, tortillas, jello, candy, and marshmallows.

Consumption of alcohol is prohibited in Islam. While perhaps not relevant to school children, it is important for teachers to know that Muslims do not drink alcoholic beverages. Likewise, foodstuffs, such as cakes, containing alcohol are unedible by Muslims.

When planning and coordinating meals, parties, or other events involving food, teachers are urged to keep the above points in mind. Muslim students can be asked to bring *halal* meat for barbeques or potlucks, for example. Also, vegetarian alternatives can be provided for Muslim students who only eat meat available directly from Muslim sources. Furthermore, dishes, baked goods, and other items that are made with vegetable shortening should be requested for such events, in order to avoid products or foods containing lard or animal shortening.

Sawm (Fasting)

During the month of *Ramadan*, the ninth month in the Islamic lunar calendar, Muslims abstain from all food and drink from dawn to sunset. This religious duty is known as *sawm* in Arabic. During this month, many Muslim students observe the fast. Consequently, these students will be unable to participate in parties or similar school events that take place during the daylight hours. Some schools also show sensitivity to fasting Muslim students by providing alternate lunch-time locations in cases where lunch is a communal meal. Muslim students may also want to abstain from rigorous physical exercise in their P.E. classes during *Ramadan*. Teachers are requested to make alternate arrangements for Muslim students, especially regarding physical education assignments.

Mixing of the Sexes

At their religious schools, at home, in various gatherings, and at social functions, Muslim men and women (and boys and girls) usually sit separately. When unmarried young men and women are together, they are accompanied by adult chaperons.

Dating, mixed-sex dancing or any form of pre-marital intimacy is not allowed in Islam. Consequently, conscientious Muslim students do not participate in proms and dances or similar events. Well-meaning school personnel sometimes put unnecessary stress on youngsters by encouraging them to participate in what they consider "normal" activities; they may even give the impression that a student who is not involved in these activities is anti-social or socially immature and needs to be coaxed into participation. The case for a Muslim student may be quite otherwise, as the student may simply be trying to act in accord with his or her religious principles and personal conscience.

For a number of reasons, including associated attire, cheerleading is another activity which does not accord with the Muslim lifestyle. Some Muslims may also refrain from participation in theatrical or dramatic presentations involving closeness or touching of members of the opposite sex. In short, any activity or function which may encourage even the least sexual innuendo or sexual tension among students is not viewed as relevant to students' purpose at school, and therefore should be avoided.

In terms of mixing in Physical Education classes, segregated sports and activities are preferred by Muslim parents. This is especially true for swimming classes.

Modesty and the Muslim Dress

Islam places great emphasis on modesty in dress and behavior. Males and females are expected to dress in clothing that does not reveal the features of the body. As part of their Islamic dress, many Muslim women and girls wear what is termed *hijab*, commonly used in reference to a scarf or headcovering, but more broadly meaning appropriate covering of the entire body except for hands, face and feet.

Physical Education classes can pose certain problems for Muslim children, since such courses typically require students to wear shorts and/or tank-tops. Such attire is not permissible for Muslim women and girls, and men and boys must wear shorts that reach at least to the knees. Teachers are requested to allow female Muslim students to wear long-sleeved t-shirts and sweatpants instead of tank-tops and shorts, and male students to wear long shorts. In addition, Muslim girls who observe *hijab* must be allowed to wear appropriate modest attire and headcovering during P.E. activities. Moreover, special swimming suits that cover more of the body should be allowed for Muslim students.

Muslims of both sexes are required to be modest even in front of persons of the same sex. Therefore, changing clothes in front of others, using the toilet or taking showers in an open area devoid of partitions or curtains presents serious problems for a Muslim youngster. Sensitive teachers and school officials may develop creative solutions to address these issues.

A FEW WORDS ABOUT HOLIDAYS

Islamic Holidays

Muslims observe two major religious holidays during the year. *Eid al-Fitr* is the celebration which occurs after *Ramadan*, while *Eid al-Adha* is the celebration which takes place at the time of the *Hajj*. On the day of *Eid*, a special worship service is held in the morning at a local *masjid* or designated gathering place. Afterwards, Muslims visit each other's homes to celebrate, share meals, and exchange gifts.

These Muslim holidays are of similar importance and significance to Muslims as are Christmas and Easter to Christians and Hanukkah and Passover to Jews. Muslim students should be given excused absences to participate in these events. Teachers are requested not to schedule any important exams or assignments on these holidays so that Muslim students can avoid any adverse effects upon their academic efforts. The *Eid* holidays (like other important dates in Islam) occur within the Islamic lunar calendar, and thus take place roughly eleven days earlier each year in relation to the standard Gregorian calendar. Teachers can obtain a calendar of Muslim holidays from local *masjids* or from various Muslim organizations, including the Council on Islamic Education.

Important Dates in the Islamic Lunar Calendar
Note: These dates are tentative since the beginning of an Islamic month is contingent upon sightability of the new moon's crescent.

Event	Islamic Date (Month, Day)	2001-2002 [1422]	2002-2003 [1423]	2003-2004 [1424]	2004-2005 [1425]
New Year begins...	Muharram 1	March 26, 2001	March 16, 2002	March 5, 2003	Feb. 23, 2004
Ramadan begins...	Ramadan 1	Nov. 17, 2001	Nov. 6, 2002	Oct. 27, 2003	Oct. 16, 2004
Eid al-Fitr	Shawwal 1	Dec. 16, 2001	Dec. 6, 2002	Nov. 25, 2003	Nov. 14, 2004
Eid al-Adha	Dhul Hijjah 10	Feb. 23, 2002	Feb. 12, 2003	Feb. 1, 2004	Jan. 21, 2005

Source: Committee for Crescent Observation, Ithaca, NY

Additional Holidays and Events

As indicated above, Muslims have two *religious* holidays. Depending on where they live in the world, Muslims may also observe or celebrate various traditional or cultural holidays and events, as long as the principles or reasons underlying them do not contradict the teachings of Islam. A brief overview of how Muslims view various events and holidays celebrated in the United States is provided below. Muslims maintain that a healthy and vibrant society is one in which uniformity is not imposed but rather differences are celebrated and appreciated.

BIRTHDAY CELEBRATIONS

Many Muslims, though not all, view the celebration of birthdays as an unhealthy or undesirable practice, since such celebrations often occupy a prominent place in one's yearly calendar, and make the "birthday person" the focus of excessive attention. Islam teaches that people should be God-conscious, moderate in their requirements, and should avoid practices which may contribute to selfishness or self-centeredness. A Muslim views the processes of birth, life, and death as originating with God. If anything, birthdays are viewed as a time for giving humble thanks to God for the gift of life and for remembering one's obligations and responsibilities, rather than a time to celebrate or receive congratulations and gifts. Usually, older Muslims refrain from any form of celebration, but birthday parties or gatherings are not uncommon for young Muslim children.

HALLOWEEN

Many Muslims view this holiday as distasteful, because of its emphasis on the macabre and supernatural. Generally, Muslims fail to see an acceptable purpose behind it, and are also concerned about possible pagan or other connotations. Consequently, some Muslim parents discourage their children from participating in "trick-or-treating," or indulging in the more morbid aspects of the event.

THANKSGIVING

The idea of thanking God for His blessings and bounty accords strongly with Islamic teachings. Many Muslim families in the United States share in the spirit of this American holiday. Traditional dinners with turkey, mashed potatoes, and pumpkin pie are a common sight in Muslim households on this holiday.

CHRISTMAS AND EASTER

Like Christians, Muslims believe in Jesus' miraculous birth and the importance of his mission. However, Muslims do not consider Jesus to have been divine. (Like all of the other prophets, he is considered a mortal creation of God.) Islam advocates uncompromising monotheism, and stresses that all worship and adoration is for God alone. Any practice which could compromise the essential principle of monotheism is forbidden or discouraged. One reason why Muslims feel that celebrating the birth or death of a prophet (whether it be Muhammad, Jesus or any other prophet), is inappropriate is that such practices may lead to *shirk*, the association of others beings with God's divinity. Thus, Muslims do not celebrate Christmas, although many participate in the spirit of goodwill towards fellow human beings.

Muslims do not believe that Jesus was crucified, but rather that he was raised to Heaven by God to spare him such a fate. Consequently, Muslims do not share the basis for the Easter celebration found in Christianity, and so do not observe this event.

Since some Muslim students may feel uncomfortable with the emphasis on Christmas during the latter part of December, they may request being excused from activities which contradict their religious beliefs, such as singing Christmas carols of a religious nature. Alternative exercises or activities should be arranged in such cases. Students also may or may not participate in Christmas gift exchanges, depending upon their individual conscience and perspective. It should be clear that these concerns do not preclude Muslim students from learning about Christmas and its importance to Christians, to which Muslims have no objection so long as appropriate ground rules for teaching about religion are employed by educators.

VALENTINE'S DAY

Islam provides specific guidelines for interaction between males and females. These guidelines are meant to enable communication in a dignified, respectful and platonic manner. The celebration of Valentine's Day is viewed by most Muslims as encouraging inappropriate sentiments between males and females, especially students near or beyond puberty. While the purpose of Valentine's Day may be to encourage positive interaction between males and females, a commendable objective, the overly idealized and romantic aura of the holiday conflicts with Islamic teachings.

MOTHER'S DAY AND FATHER'S DAY

Great emphasis is placed on the family unit in Islam. Muslims have a religious obligation to respect, love, and honor their parents and elders at all times. Thus, the purpose of Mother's Day and Father's Day accords well with the religious beliefs of Muslims, and many Muslims participate in this holiday in various ways. At the same time, Muslims caution that exhibiting greater care and affection for one's parents on one particular day during the year may inadvertently reinforce a notion among youngsters which undermines the constant form of care and companionship which is necessary to build strong, constructive, and loving bonds between parents and children.

OTHER CULTURAL HOLIDAYS

Muslims around the world have many different cultures and nationalities. Consequently, some Muslims, in addition to celebrating the religious holidays, may participate in specific cultural festivals, such as the Chinese New Year, or Nau-roz (Persian New Year). Many American Muslims, like their fellow citizens and residents, may participate in or observe Independence Day, Memorial Day, Veteran's Day, and other celebrations or events.

Recommended Resources

The Council on Islamic Education recognizes that educators are faced with enormous challenges in teaching about world religions in an accurate, balanced and sensitive manner. When it comes to Islam, these challenges are augmented due to popular misconceptions and stereotypes, reliance on outdated, unbalanced or superficial sources, and a paucity of readily-usable resources, hands-on materials and teaching tools. This condition unfortunately applies to many books and sources currently available at public libraries, and consequently they contain dated insights, statistics, and visual images. Moreover, these materials often fail to adequately address contemporary issues and circumstances. Even bookstores, despite their emphasis on acquiring the most recently published materials, may not always carry works on Islam that are widely considered accurate, or that are readily usable by educators and others looking for adequate reference materials.

In order to avoid perpetuating inaccuracies and misunderstanding, educators need access to books and materials which provide clear, substantive information on Islam, as well as on a variety of subtopics and issues related to Islam, Muslims, and Muslim history and culture. The following list of books and resources, recommended by scholars and educators nationwide, provides a solid introduction to the topic, and fosters the educator's efforts towards teaching about Islam in the public school classroom. An effort has been made to include only those materials with direct relevance or usefulness to the classroom, and therefore the list is neither exhaustive nor representative of the full spectrum of sources available. Rather, this listing is meant as a guide to help educators eliminate the usual guesswork involved in selecting worthwhile materials. We hope the listed works will be of value to the broadest range of educators. Some sources will be of interest to Muslim educators and parents as well.

Items are grouped under the following general categories: *Reading and Reference Resources*, *Teaching Resources*, *Video and Audio Resources*, and *Computer Resources*. Grade-level appropriateness, and other characteristics are indicated for selected works. Following the various categories of recommended resources is a section listing materials not recommended for use in the classroom. A list of resource organizations is provided at the end in order to facilitate teachers' acquisition of recommended items.

READING AND REFERENCE RESOURCES

Introduction to Islam

Abu Ghosh, Bassam Sulaiman
and Waffa Zaki Shaqra
A Glossary of Islamic Terminology
London: TaHa Publishers, 1992.

*A handy reference book containing definitions for
a plethora of Arabic words and terms related to
Islam and Muslims.*

Al-Faruqi, Isma'il R.
Islam
Beltsville, MD: Amana Publications, 1994.
83pp. ISBN: 0-89505-022-6

*An insightful and eloquent overview of Islam by
one of the most renowned Muslim scholars of the
20th century, the late professor Isma'il Al-Faruqi.
Highly recommended.*

DuPasquier, Roger
Unveiling Islam
Cambridge, U.K.: Islamic Texts Society, 1992.
157pp. ISBN: 0-946621-32-2

*Beyond covering the basics of Islamic belief and
practice, this book explores philosophical and
religious approaches to humankind's contemporary
plight, with emphasis on Islam's guidelines for
fostering a righteous society.*

Esposito, John
Islam - The Straight Path
New York: Oxford University Press, 1988.
230pp. ISBN: 0-19-504399-5

*An accessible, thorough overview of Islam and
Muslims, written by a well-known contemporary
scholar. Available in many bookstores nationwide.*

Farah, Caesar
Islam
Hauppauge, NY: Barrons Educational Series,
1994. 434pp. ISBN: 0-8120-1853-2

*A useful addition to the "Introduction to Islam"
genre. Provides details about the advent of Islam,
its spread, and contemporary issues facing the
worldwide Muslim community.*

Glassé, Cyril
The Concise Encyclopedia of Islam
San Francisco: HarperCollins, 1989.
472pp. ISBN: 0-06-063126-0

*An excellent reference book that should be in every
educator's personal library. Extremely
comprehensive coverage of a vast number of topics
from the realms of theology, history, science,
philosophy, and practice.*

Haneef, Suzanne
**What Everyone Should Know
About Islam and Muslims**
Chicago: Kazi Publications, 1985.
195pp. ISBN: 0-935782-00-1

*A straightforward approach towards explaining the
religion of Islam and its adherents. Particularly
useful as it explores life for Muslims in the United
States and the challenges that young Muslims face
growing up in the American cultural milieu.*

Khan, Nafisa
Light Upon Light
Ottawa, Canada: Wake-Robin Inc., 1987.
119pp. ISBN: 0-9693253-0-4

*A simple yet engaging introduction to Islam, with
lots of color photographs. Especially useful is a
section containing Qur'anic verses about topics
such as "The Soul," "Men and Women," and
"Death and Resurrection."*

Maqsood, Ruqaiyyah
Teach Yourself Islam
Chicago: NTC Publishing Group, 1994.
218pp. ISBN: 0-86316-155-3

*A straightforward and refreshing overview of Islam,
with emphasis on contemporary issues and
lifestyles. Topics covered include Muslim
minorities, crime and punishment, marriage and
sexual relations, views on youth and old age, among
others. This book is part of the "Teach Yourself...."
series which covers all of the world's
major religions.*

Matar, N.I.
Islam for Beginners
New York: Writers and Readers Publishing, 1992. 196pp. ISBN: 0-86316-155-3

A fun, highly informative overview of Islam and Muslim history, with plenty of graphics and illustrations throughout. Designed in an almost comic book style, making it easy and enjoyable to read.

Rahman, Fazlur
Islam
Chicago: University of Chicago Press, 1979. 285pp. ISBN: 0-226-70281-2

An interesting and thorough overview of Islam and Muslim history. This work has been updated several times since its original publication in order to remain current.

Renard, John
In the Footsteps of Muhammad - Understanding the Islamic Experience
New York: Paulist Press, 1992. 173pp. ISBN: 0-8091-3316-4

A detailed and sensitive overview. Includes a section on Islam in America. Well-written, with clearly organized topics.

Sardar, Ziauddin and Zafar Abbas Malik
Introducing Muhammad
New York: Totem Books, 1994. 176pp. ISBN: 1-874166-15-3 $9.95

A very light-hearted yet effective approach towards introducing Islam. The pages are choke-full of graphics, illustrations, quotes, and facts and figures. An excellent source for teachers and others.

Schimmel, Annemarie
Islam - An Introduction
New York: State University of New York Press, 1992. 166pp. ISBN: 0-7914-1328-4

An excellent survey of the Muslim faith and the diverse spiritual expressions found in Islam, by a noted scholar in the field. Very insightful.

Williams, John Alden
The Word of Islam
Austin: University of Texas Press, 1994. ISBN: 0-292-7073-2

An attempt to let Islam speak for itself through its own authoritative texts. Recommended.

Zepp, Ira G.
A Muslim Primer - Beginner's Guide to Islam
Westminster, MD: Wakefield Editions, 1992. 292pp. ISBN: 0-87061-188-7

A useful guide to Muslim belief and practice. Written with special emphasis on Muslim-Christian interreligious understanding and dialogue.

The Qur'an and Commentaries

Ali, Abdullah Yusuf, tr.
The Meaning of the Holy Qur'an
Beltsville, MD: Amana Publications, 1994.

A very popular and widely-read translation and commentary on the Qur'an. Includes Arabic script and English translation. The English text is written in a highly formal, 17th-century English style.

Asad, Muhammad, tr.
The Message of the Qur'an
Gibraltar, Spain: Dar al-Andalus, 1980. ISBN: 0-317-5245-9

A highly recommended translation of the Qur'an, with extensive explanatory footnotes. Contains original Arabic script and English translation in a contemporary style.

Cleary, Thomas, tr.
The Essential Qur'an
San Francisco: HarperCollins, 1994. 203pp. ISBN: 0-06-250198-4

A lucid and thought-provoking translation and analysis of selected verses from the Qur'an. Useful for those interested in exploring the core concepts of the scripture.

Cortes, Julio, tr.
El Coran
Chicago: Kazi Publications, 1987.
ISBN: 1-56744-440-7

A Spanish translation of the Qur'an. Contains original Arabic script and Spanish translation side-by-side. Particularly useful for bilingual educators.

Irving, Thomas B., tr.
The Qur'an - First American Version
Beltsville, MD: Amana Books, 1991.
400pp. ISBN: 0-915597-81-0

The first translation of the Qur'an in contemporary American English. Contains both Arabic script and English translation.

Kazi, Mazhar
A Glimpse into the Glorious Qur'an
Plainfield, IN: American Trust Publications, 1986. ISBN: 0-89259-059-9

A handy compilation of verses from the Qur'an, arranged according to subject. For example, verses related to fasting are grouped together under one heading, as are verses for other topics, such as "Day of Judgment," "Forgiveness," and "Drinking and Gambling."

Osman, Fathi
Concepts of the Qur'an: A Topical Reading
Los Angeles: MVI Publications, 1997.
ISBN: 1-881504-42-5

An insightful and handy reference work which enables readers to study specific Qur'anic passages which pertain to larger themes that run throughout the sacred text. Topics covered include the faith of Islam itself, types of worship, moral values and manners, the Islamic law, among others.

Pickthall, Muhammad Marmaduke, tr.
The Meaning of the Glorious Koran
New York: Mentor Group, 1953.
464pp. ISBN: 0-451-62745-8

A highly-regarded translation of the Qur'an, with extensive explanatory footnotes. Contains Arabic script and ornate English translation.

Note: Translations in various languages are available, including Chinese, Vietnamese, Bosnian, French, German, Spanish, and Urdu, among others. Consult the resource organizations listed at the end of this section for further information.

Hadith

Al-Sahrawardy, Allama Sir Abdullah, tr.
The Sayings of Muhammad
New York: Citadel Press, 1990.
128pp. ISBN: 0-8065-01169-9

A pocket-book sized reference. Contains a diverse and insightful selection from among the thousands of authentic sayings of Prophet Muhammad.

Cleary, Thomas, tr.
The Wisdom of the Prophet - Sayings of Muhammad
Boston: Shambala Press, 1994.
ISBN: 1-57062-017-2 $6.00

A selection of universal teachings of Prophet Muhammad, taken from his recorded hadith. Very handy pocket-book format.

Hadith
London: Umran Publications, 1981.
ISBN: 0-907757-00-6

A beautifully produced book containing some of the personal sayings of Prophet Muhammad. Each page contains a full-page black-and-white photograph depicting the daily life of Muslims, which serves as a backdrop for a particular hadith.

Siddiqi, Muhammad Zubayr
Hadith Literature - Its Origin, Development and Special Features
Cambridge, U.K.: Islamic Texts Society, 1993.
174pp. ISBN: 0-946621-38-1

For those interested in the science of hadith, the process by which hadith were recorded, transmitted, and collected by scholars in the years following Prophet Muhammad's death, this work provides substantial insight.

Life of Muhammad

Armstrong, Karen
Muhammad - A Biography of the Prophet
New York: HarperCollins, 1992.
290pp. ISBN: 0-06-250886-5

A sensitive, interesting account of Prophet Muhammad's life, written by a renowned author. Especially valuable is this book's effort to place Islam in proper historical context, high-lighting its salient features as the last of the great monotheistic religions.

Azzam, Abd al-Rahman
Eternal Message of Muhammad
Cambridge, U.K.: Islamic Texts Society, 1993.
297pp. ISBN: 0-946621-48-9

This work goes beyond an account of the Prophet's life to discuss the impact of his teachings on world history since the advent of Islam. Particular attention is paid to social reform, the Muslim state, international relations, and the ramifications of colonialism for Muslim society. Highly recommended.

Haykal, Muhammad H.
The Life of Muhammad
Plainfield, IN: American Trust Publications, 1976. 639pp. ISBN: 0-89259-002-5

An excellent source on the life of Prophet Muhammad. His early life, call to prophethood and subsequent leadership of the emerging Muslim community are examined in detail. An important reference for educators.

Lings, Martin
Muhammad - His Life Based on the Earliest Sources
New York: Inner Traditions International, Ltd., 1983. 360pp. ISBN: 0-89281-170-6

An excellent biography of Prophet Muhammad, written in an engaging narrative style.. Each major historical event of Prophet Muhammad's mission is discussed in a chapter two to six pages in length, providing a useful format for reading and research.

Rahman, Afzalur
Muhammad - Encyclopedia of Seerah
Leicester, U.K.: Seerah Foundation, 1981.
Eight volumes. ISBN: 0-907052-14-2

A comprehensive, definitive source on many aspects of Prophet Muhammad's life. Explores not only his role as messenger of God, but also as model leader, husband, father, and friend. This multi-volume work also contains substantial background on pre-Islamic Arabian history, as well as Muslim history since the advent of Islam. Highly recommended for school libraries and honors classes.

Sardar, Ziauddin
Muhammad - Aspects of His Biography
Leicester, U.K.: The Islamic Foundation, 1978.
67pp. ISBN: 0-86037-023-2

A brief, well-written account of the life of Muhammad. Contains many pictures, illustrations, and maps of seventh-century Arabia.

Siddiqui, A.H.
Life of Muhammad
Des Plaines, IL: Library of Islam, 1991.
324pp. ISBN: 0-934905-21-5

A useful addition to this genre of books. Written in a clear, straightforward style.

Biographies of Muslims

Ahmad, K.J.
Hundred Great Muslims
Chicago: Library of Islam, 1987.
573pp. ISBN: 0-933511-16-7

A handy reference on selected Muslim historical figures. Contains biographical information on diverse important personages, including rulers, scientists, artisans, poets, and statesmen.

Athar, Alia N.
Prophets - Models for Humanity
Chicago: Library of Islam, 1993.
229pp. ISBN: 1-56744-425-3

Provides a brief account of the life and character of thirty prophets of God, based on information found in Islamic sources and in the Muslim scholarly tradition. Prophets discussed include Adam, Noah, Abraham, Ishmael, Isaac, Joseph, Moses, David, Zachariah, John, Jesus, and Muhammad.

Bakhtiar, Laleh
Muhammad's Companions - Essays on Some Who Bore Witness to His Message
Chicago: Library of Islam, 1993.
210pp. ISBN: 1-56744-426-1

Explores the character and personality of several of Prophet Muhammad's companions. Persons covered include Khadijah (his first wife), Bilal Ibn Rabah (the first mueddhin), and the pious caliphs, among others.

El-Shabazz, Malik (Malcolm X) and Alex Haley
The Autobiography of Malcolm X
New York: Ballantine Books, 1965.
460pp. ISBN: 0-345-35068-5

El-Hajj Malik El-Shabazz, commonly known as Malcolm X, renounced beliefs advocated by the Nation of Islam, a nationalist organization, and entered the fold of mainstream Islam after performing the Hajj in 1963. In this book, he tells of his remarkable story of transformation from childhood until right before his assassination in February, 1965.

Hamid, Abdul Wahid
Companions of the Prophet
London: Umran Publications, 1982.
125pp. ISBN: 0-907757-02-2

An excellent source on twenty of the Prophet's companions, some famous, others not so well known. Based on original Arabic sources and written in a lively narrative style.

Mernissi, Fatima
The Forgotten Queens of Islam
Minneapolis, MN: University of Minnesota Press, 1993. 229pp. ISBN: 0-8166-2438-0

This work brings to light from the shadows of history the lives of fifteen important and influential Muslim women. The stories of these diverse and interesting persons provide insight into Muslim societies past and present.

Muslim Society and Culture

Ahmed, Akbar
Living Islam - From Samarkand to Stornoway
New York: Facts on File, 1992.
224pp. ISBN: 0-8160-1303-7

A compendium of facts, figures, photographs and anecdotes designed to bring the diversity of the Muslim community to life. Besides providing historical overviews of Muslim societies, the author delves into issues of modernity, interreligious relations, and media coverage of Islam.

Ahsan, A. H.
Muslim Festivals
Vero Beach, FL: Rourke Enterprises, 1987.
ISBN: 0-86592-979-3

A concise and straightforward overview of Muslim religious holidays and the observances associated with them. Useful for enhancing teachers' awareness of their Muslim students' needs.

Al-Faruqi, Ismail and Lamya Faruqi
Cultural Atlas of Islam
New York: MacMillan Publishing Co., 1986.
512pp. ISBN: 0-02-910190-5

A extremely valuable resource that provides information on numerous aspects of Muslim culture and history, such as calligraphy, music, and literature. Contains many unique photographs, maps, and illustrations. Recommended for schools.

Al-Qaradawi, Yusuf
The Lawful and the Prohibited in Islam
Plainfield, IN: American Trust Publications, 1989. 353pp. ISBN: 0-85630-016-5

What foods are lawful for Muslims? What forms of employment are acceptable in Islam? Whom may one marry as a Muslim? These and many other issues are addressed in this comprehensive reference by a renowned scholar.

Burckhardt, Titus
Fez - City of Islam
Cambridge, U.K.: Islamic Texts Society, 1992.
ISBN: 0-946621-17-9

An interesting photo-book about one of the most important cities in Muslim history. Extensive discussion of North African Muslim cultures and lifestyles.

Diouf, Sylviane
Servants of Allah: African Muslims Enslaved in the Americas
New York: New York University Press, 1998. 545pp. ISBN: 0-814-7190-58

An insightful and deeply researched portrait of early American Muslim life. Traces the struggles of African slaves who professed Islam.

Haddad, Yvonne Y. and Jane I Smith, eds.
Muslim Communities in North America
New York: State University of New York Press, 1994. 545pp. ISBN: 0-7914-2020-5

A recent study of the diverse Muslim community in the United States and Canada. Contains useful facts and figures, and an overview of American Muslim history.

Hasan, Asma Gull
American Muslims
New York: Continuum, 2001. 200pp. ISBN: 0-8264-1362-5

An insightful, humorous and lively account of one American Muslim's experience growing up in America. A fresh look at many current issues.

Hathout, Hassan
Reading the Muslim Mind
Plainfield, IN: American Trust Publications, 1995. 152pp. ISBN: 0-89259-157-9

An eloquent, fascinating tour through the Islamic way of life, emphasizing the mindset behind the practice and the spirit behind the letter. Recommended.

Hussaini, M.H. and Ahmad H. Sakr
Islamic Dietary Laws and Practices
Chicago: Islamic Food and Nutrition Council of America, 1983. 165pp.
Library of Congress No. 83-082107

This book is appropriate for those interested in the details of Muslim dietary practice. Contains discussion of health issues and the role of diet upon the physiological and spiritual components of human existence. Also contains many recipes for traditional Muslim dishes from various cultures.

Kamali, Mohammad Hashim
Principles of Islamic Jurisprudence
Cambridge, U.K.: Islamic Texts Society, 1991. 417pp. ISBN: 0-946621-24-1

Those interested in an in-depth, authoritative study of the development of Shari'ah (Islamic Law) and its application in jurisprudence will find this a thought-provoking source. Also contains discussion of modern tendencies in Islamic legal theory.

Kazi, Marian
Adhan Over Anatolia - Diary of an American Muslim
Plainfield, IN: American Trust Publications. 211pp. ISBN: 0-87141-054-0

An interesting contemporary account of the experiences and impressions of an American Muslim woman and her family in Europe and Turkey. Readers gain particular insight regarding the roles of culture and religion in the Anatolian province.

Lings, Martin
What is Sufism?
Cambridge, U.K.: Islamic Texts Society, 1993. 133pp. ISBN: 0-946621-41-1

A good introductory source on the ideas embodied in Sufism, a form of exemplary spiritual devotion practiced by Muslims from various walks of life.

Mohamed, Mamdouh N.
Hajj and Umrah — From A to Z
Mamdouh N. Mohamed, 1996. 92pp. ISBN: 0-915957-54-X

An extremely well-designed guidebook for the pilgrimage to Makkah. Contains numerous graphics, illustrations and charts in conjunction with a user-friendly step-by-step account of the pilgrimage acts and events. Very comprehensive.

Momen, Moojan
An Introduction to Shi'i Islam
New Haven, CT: Yale University Press, 1985. 397pp. ISBN: 0-300-03531-4

Exhaustive overview of the origins and branches of Shi'i Islam. Useful reference.

Muslim World Cook Book

Plainfield, IN: American Trust Publications, 1976. 134pp.

A wonderful compilation of recipes from throughout the Muslim world. Includes chapters on soups and side dishes, breads, beverages, meat and fish, rice dishes, and desserts.

Nasr, Seyyed Hossein
Ideals and Realities of Islam

London: Allen and Unwin, 1966. 188pp. ISBN: 0-04-297049-0

An important work by a renowned American Muslim scholar. This work explores Islamic principles designed to foster human excellence, and the factors which separate ideal practice from the spectrum of actual practice.

Nawwab, Ismail, et al.
Aramco and Its World: Arabia and the Middle East

Dahran, Saudi Arabia: Aramco, 1980. 275pp.

A valuable reference, containing information on life, culture, religion, commerce, industrialization, and modernization in the Middle East. Contains lots of maps, illustrations and photographs.

Nyang, Sulayman
Islam in the United States of America

Chicago: Kazi Publications, 1999. 165pp.

A useful and reliable overvew of the growth of the Muslim community in the United States. Written by one of the foremost experts on the subject.

Osman, Fathi
Sharia in Contemporary Society - The Dynamics of Change in the Islamic Law

Los Angeles, CA: Multimedia Vera International, 1994. 146pp. ISBN: 1-881504-07-7

A concise, cogent work on the application of Shari'ah (Islamic Law) in contemporary times. This book endeavors to distinguish between that which is divine and permanent and that which is human and changeable in the Islamic legal heritage.

Sabbagh, Isa Khalil
As The Arabs Say...

Washington D.C.: Sabbagh Management Corp., 1983. Two volumes. ISBN: 0-912369-00-0 and 0-912369-01-0

A beautifully-produced labor of love by a renowned entrepreneur and diplomat. Contains numerous Arabic and Islamic quotations, in a handsome calligraphic style, along with insightful yet light-hearted explanatory text.

Smith, Jane I. and Yvonne Y. Haddad
Islamic Understanding of Death and Resurrection

New York: State University of New York Press, 1981. 262pp. ISBN: 0-87395-507-2

Belief in the Hereafter is a fundamental component of Islam. This book sheds light on Islam's teachings regarding death and that which human beings experience subsequently.

Family and Gender Issues

Ahmed, Leila
Women and Gender in Islam

New Haven, CT: Yale University Press, 1992. 296pp. ISBN: 0-300-05583-8

Covers the role of women in Middle Eastern society from pre-Islamic to modern times. Special emphasis on new discourses on the topic that have developed in recent times.

Al-Faruqi, Lamya
Women, Muslim Society, and Islam

Plainfield, IN: American Trust Publications. 1991. 78pp. ISBN: 0-89259-068-8

Discusses a wide range of issues, such as marriage, divorce, gender roles, feminism, legal rights, education, and the family model. Well-written and concise.

Ebrahim, Abul Fadl Mohsin
Abortion, Birth Control and Surrogate Parenting - An Islamic Perspective

Plainfield, IN: American Trust Publications, 1989. 103pp. ISBN: 0-89259-081-5

An important source for Muslims' views on various contemporary reproductive issues. Extensive use of sources and references from the Islamic scholarly tradition.

El-Amin, Mildred M.
Family Roots - The Qur'anic View of Family Life
Chicago: Intl. Ummah Foundation, 1991.
242pp. ISBN: 0-911119-38-8

An interesting and informative work that sheds light on the Muslim viewpoint regarding many family, health, and gender issues. Written by a Muslim American in a question and answer format.

Esposito, John
Women in Muslim Family Law
Syracuse, NY: Syracuse University Press, 1982.
155pp. ISBN: 0-8156-2278-3

An honest and sensitive exploration of the scriptural and legal basis for gender equality in Islam. Explains how laws based on Shari'ah take into consideration differences between the two sexes, and how such laws function in Muslim societies.

Hamid, Azieza
The Book of Muslim Names
London: Muslim Education and Literary Services, 1985. 47pp. ISBN: 0-948196-03-3

Useful handbook containing several hundred Muslim names and their meanings. The introduction explains the importance of names to Muslims, giving educators further insight into the Muslim worldview.

Kahf, Mohja
Western Representations of the Muslim Woman
Austin: University of Texas Press, 1999. 224pp. ISBN: 0-2927-4336X

The author has made an intriguing analysis of the ways in which the idea of the Muslim woman has figured in Western literature, plays, songs, and the popular imagination.

Mutahhari, Murtaza and Laleh Bakhtiar
Hijab - The Islamic Modest Dress
Chicago: Kazi Publications, 1989.
ISBN: 1-87103-15-X

Explains the Islamic concept of modesty and how it translates into modest attire. A useful resource.

Stowasser, Barbara F.
Women in the Qur'an, Traditions, and Interpretation
New York: Oxford University Press, 1994.
206pp. ISBN: 0-19-508480-2

Explores the Islamic sources for information on several important female historical figures, including the wives of Prophet Muhammad, Bilqis (the Queen of Sheba), Eve, and Mary. An engaging resource for gender studies.

Wudud-Mohsin, Amina
Qur'an and Woman
Kuala Lumpur, Malaysia: Penerbrit Fajar Bakti Sdu. Bhd., 1992.
118pp. ISBN: 967-65-1976-6

An excellent, erudite work. Provides in-depth analysis of various Qur'anic chapters and verses that pertain to women, and contrasts various interpretations on the subject.

History and Politics

Adas, Michael, ed.
Islamic and European Expansion - The Forging of a Global Order
Philadelphia: Temple University Press, 1993.
379pp. ISBN: 1-56639-068-0

This book, containing ten articles from top-notch scholars, sheds light upon the historical interrelationships of the Muslim and European civilizations, often unrecognized or neglected in typical sources. Useful for comparative studies.

Ahmad, Mumtaz, ed.
State Politics and Islam
Plainfield, IN: American Trust Publications, 1986. 160pp. ISBN: 0-89259-058-0

Each chapter in this work has been written by a different Muslim scholar. Topics include Islamic political theory, appointment of the head of state, legislation, and social justice. Recommended for political science enthusiasts.

Ahmed, Akbar S.
**Discovering Islam -
Making Sense of Muslim History and Society**
London: Routledge Inc., 1988.
251pp. ISBN: 0-415-03930-4

An interesting work designed to bridge the gap between Muslim history and contemporary Muslim societies. Helps provide context for many present-day issues and events.

Ahmed, Akbar S.
Postmodernism and Islam
London: Routledge Inc., 1992.
ISBN: 0-14-023341-5

An exploration of Islam and its role as a spiritual beacon in a postmodern world steeped in cynicism, violence, technology and emotional isolation.

Ahsan, Muhammad M.
Social Life Under the Abbasids, 786-902 AD
London: Longman Group, 1979.
316pp.

This work provides insight into the increasingly sophisticated urban life which gained momentum during the Abbasid period (750 - 1258 C.E.) of Muslim history. A useful tool for cross-cultural historical comparisons.

Amin, Samir
Eurocentrism
New York: Monthly Review Press, 1989.
152pp. ISBN: 0-85345-786-7

A study of the historical discourse and dissemination of information that developed with the rise to prominence of Europe, and which continues to play a role in academic approaches to history and related disciplines.

Bezirgan, Basima and Elizabeth Fernea, eds.
Middle Eastern Women Speak
Austin: University of Texas Press, 1977.
399pp. ISBN: 0-292-75041-2

A interesting, insightful collection of autobiographical and biographical writings by and about Middle Eastern women. Historical figures as well as contemporary persons are included.

Chejne, Anwar
Islam and the West: The Moriscos
New York: State University of New York Press, 1984. 248pp. ISBN: 0-87395-606-0

An important work designed to show the interconnections between Islam and Western civilization, particularly in terms of the experiences of Moriscos (Muslims living under Christian rule in Spain). Interesting information on the culture, art and architecture of the Moriscos.

Cleveland, William
A History of the Modern Middle East
Boulder, CO: Westview Press, 1994.
503pp. ISBN: 0-8133-0563-2

A new, well-written and balanced treatment of Middle Eastern history. Extensive coverage of the Ottoman and Safavid empires, the transformation of Egypt and Iran in the nineteenth century, and World Wars I and II. Includes information up to 1993. Recommended.

Cohen, Mark
**Under Crescent and Cross -
The Jews of the Middle Ages**
Princeton, NJ: Princeton University Press, 1994. 280pp.

An interesting historical comparison of Jewish experience in Muslim and Christian lands. Explores the Islamic concept of "ahl al-kitab" and its ramifications for Jews in the Middle Ages living under Muslim rule.

Daftary, Farhad
The Isma'ilis - Their History and Doctrines
Cambridge: Cambridge University Press, 1990.
804pp. ISBN: 81-215-0494-X

A comprehensive overview of Isma'ili Shi'i origins, history and doctrines.

Esposito, John L.
The Islamic Threat - Myth or Reality?
New York: Oxford University Press, 1992.
247pp. ISBN: 0-19-508666-X

Challenges prevailing myths and stereotypes about the resurgence of Islam in the Muslim world. Explores issues of religious revival, modernity, transformation, human rights, representative government (or lack thereof) and so-called "fundamentalism."

Gabrieli, Francesco
Arab Historians of the Crusades
New York: Dorset Press, 1957.
362pp. ISBN: 0-88029-452-3

A view of the Crusades from the "other side." For the Muslims of the time, the arrival of waves of Crusaders was seen as nothing less than an invasion. Find out what various chroniclers had to say about the Christian forces and the Muslim response.

Holmes, George, ed.
The Oxford Illustrated History of Medieval Europe
Oxford, U.K.: Oxford University Press, 1988.
398pp. ISBN: 0-19820-073-0

A useful reference for cross-cultural historical comparisons. Particularly valuable for teachers wanting to illustrate Muslim civilization in relation to Europe during the "Middle Ages."

Hourani, Albert
Europe and the Middle East
Berkeley: University of California Press, 1980.
226pp. ISBN: 0-52003-742-1

Explores the many interconnections between the European and Middle Eastern civilizations. Provides interesting information on contributions of Muslims that helped foster the emergence of Europe in the modern era.

Hourani, Albert
A History of the Arab Peoples
New York: Warner Books, 1992.
549pp. ISBN: 0-446-39392-4

A classic work overflowing with insightful commentary and analysis. This resource discusses pre-Islamic Arabia, the forging of a new order with the advent of Islam, the development of Arab Muslim societies, the Ottoman period, the era of European empires, and the age of the nation-state.

Izetbegovic, Alija
Islam Between East and West
Plainfield, IN: American Trust Publications, 1984. 291pp. ISBN: 0-89259-057-2

Provides insight into the practice of Islam in Eastern Europe, and the challanges faced by Muslims living between the Soviet and Western realms. Written by the current President of Bosnia-Hercegovina.

Krejcí, Jaroslav
Before the European Challenge - The Great Civilizations of Asia and the Middle East
New York: State University of New York Press, 1989. 348pp. ISBN: 0-7914-0169-3

For a more global approach to world history, teachers need sources that shed light on various civilizations. This book is ideal for a comprehensive, comparative history survey.

Köszegi, Michael and J. Gordon Melton, eds.
Islam In North America - A Sourcebook
New York: Garland Press, 1992.
392pp. ISBN: 0-8153-0918-X

First-of-its-kind research tool. Features articles from numerous outstanding American Muslim scholars, and includes information on Muslim organizations, African-American Muslims, and other topics. Invaluable addition to any school library.

Lapidus, Ira M.
A History of Islamic Societies
Cambridge, U.K.: Cambridge University Press, 1990. 1002pp. ISBN: 0-52122-552-3

A comprehensive approach to Muslim history, focusing on the histories of individual Muslim cultural/ethnic societies. A standard reference work.

Lapidus, Ira M.
Muslim Cities in the Later Middle Ages
Cambridge, U.K.: Cambridge University Press, 1967. 208pp. Library of Congress No. 66021339

Explore the layout, function and features of Muslim cities of the recent past. An intriguing look into the ideas and religious imperatives that shape the Muslim urban environment.

Maalouf, Amin
The Crusades Through Arab Eyes
New York: Schocken Books, Inc., 1984.
295pp. ISBN: 0-8052-0898-4

An interesting and valuable resource for educators teaching about the complex circumstances and motivations surrounding the Crusades. Useful for providing students with an inclusive, multifaceted view of history.

Muhammad, Al-Hajj Wali Akbar
**Muslims in Georgia -
A Chronology & Oral History**
Fayetteville, GA: The Brandon Institute, 1993.

Interesting look into facts and events related to the presence of Muslims in Georgia. Contains recollections of persons, biographical sketches, and other useful information.

Makdisi, George
**The Rise of Colleges -
Institutions of Learning in Islam and the West**
New York: State University of New York Press, 1981. 377pp. ISBN: 0-87395-455-6

Insightful look at the development of educational institutions in the Muslim world, and the impact of such institutions on emerging European forms. Useful for comparative history.

Nasr, Seyyed Hossein, Hamid Dabashi, and Seyyed V.R. Nasr, eds.
Shi'ism - Doctrines, Thought and Spirituality
New York: State University of New York Press, 1988. 401pp. ISBN: 0-88706-690-9

A collection of essays on various aspects of Shi'ism. Useful for a broader understanding of Shi'ah history and thought.

Peters, F.E.
A Reader on Classical Islam
Princeton, NJ: Princeton University Press, 1994. 420pp. ISBN: 0-691-00040-9

Cogent coverage of Muslims' views on the prophetic tradition, the life of Muhammad, the Qur'an as Word of God, and other salient elements of Islamic belief and practice. Highly recommended.

Powell, James M.
Muslims Under Latin Rule
Princeton, NJ: Princeton University Press, 1990. 221pp.

A useful exploration of the Muslim experience under Latin Christian rule. Interesting source for information on Spain after Muslim rule.

Robinson, Francis
Atlas of the Islamic World Since 1500
New York: Facts on File, 1982.
238pp. ISBN: 0-87196-629-8 $35.00

A colorful and informative source on the recent history of Muslim societies. Contains articles on colonialism, modernization, and related topics, along with photographs, maps, charts, and figures.

Said, Edward
Covering Islam
New York: Pantheon Books, 1981.
186pp. ISBN: 0-394-74808-5

Provides an overview of the factors and dynamics involved in the coverage of Islam in news media, film, and other sources of information.

Said, Edward
Orientalism
New York: Vintage Books, 1978.
368pp. ISBN: 0-394-74067-X

This classic work by Edward Said provides an in-depth and thought-provoking analysis of the relationship between the West and the Muslim world, and the academic phenomenon known as Orientalism. Recommended for high school honors teachers and students.

Semaan, Khalil I., ed.
**Islam and the Medieval West -
Aspects of Intercultural Relations**
New York: State University of New York Press, 1979. 172pp. ISBN: 0-87395-409-2

An important study of the interconnections between the two civilizations most directly responsible for the modern world. Recommended for teachers interested in comparative history.

Sonyel, Salahi Ramadan
The Muslims of Bosnia
Leicester, U.K.: The Islamic Foundation, 1994.
72pp. ISBN: 0-86037-238-3

For teachers wishing to give students greater insight into the history and culture of Bosnia, and who want to study the circumstances leading to and perpetuating the genocide of Bosnian Muslims. Especially useful for "Current Events" courses.

Watt, W. Montgomery and Pierre Cachia
A History of Islamic Spain
Edinburgh, U.K.: Edinburgh University Press, 1965. 210pp. ISBN: 0-85224-3324

Muslim Spain was an important bridge between the Muslim lands of the East and Europe. Explore the history and culture of al-Andalus (the Arabic name for what is now Spain), the interrelations between Muslims, Jews, and Christians in Spain, and other facets of the unique society documented in this well-written book.

Watt, W. Montgomery
Islamic Surveys:
The Influence of Islam on Medieval Europe
Edinburgh, U.K.: Edinburgh University Press, 1972. ISBN: 0-85224-439-8.

A valuable source for more complete historical surveys. Draws connections between Muslim civilization and Europe, emphasizing scientific methodology, intellectual tradition, and other factors contributing to European prominence.

Science and Civilization

Al-Hassan, Ahmad and Donald Hill
Islamic Technology - An Illustrated History
Cambridge, U.K.: Cambridge University Press, 1986. 304pp. ISBN: 0-521-42239-6

This book emphasizes the historical application of scientific knowledge to technology in the Muslim civilization. Lavishly illustrated with line-drawings and photographs throughout.

Athar, Shahid, ed.
Islamic Perspectives in Medicine
Plainfield, IN: American Trust Publications, 1993. 220pp. ISBN: 089259-141-2

Study the basis for medical research and training in Islam. This work, containing numerous articles by physicians and scientists, documents the philosophical and theological approaches of Muslims to medicine and some of their contributions to the field.

Bucaille, Dr. Maurice
What Is The Origin of Man?
Paris: Seghers Inc., 1984.
219pp. ISBN: 2-221-01101-5

Discusses evolution, cellular organization, natural selection, genetics, and other related issues from both a scientific and scriptural point-of-view. Thought-provoking.

Gies, Frances and Joseph
Cathedral, Forge and Waterwheel -
Technology and Invention in the Middle Ages
New York: HarperCollins, 1994.

An interesting work on the evolution of technology in the Middle Ages, highlighting those inventions, some of which were developed by Muslims, of greatest import.

Gruner, O. Cameron, tr.
The Canon of Medicine of Avicenna *(Ibn Sina)*
London: Luzac & Co., 1930. 612pp.

Ibn Sina (b. 980 C.E.) was one of the most renowned scientists and thinkers in world history. This book contains a treatise on the first of Ibn Sina's famous five-volume work.

Hayes, John R., ed.
The Genius of Arab Civilization -
Source of Renaissance
Cambridge, MA: MIT Press, 1983.
260pp. ISBN: 0-262-58063-2

Provides meaningful discussion of the relationship between Muslim science and civilization and the Renaissance that took place subsequently in 15th and 16th century Europe.

Imamuddin, S.M.
Arabic Writing and Arab Libraries
London: TaHa Publishers, 1983.
80pp. ISBN: 0-907461-29-8

An interesting exploration of the development of libraries in Muslim civilization. Includes discussion of Arabic writing methods, language development, and calligraphy forms. Provides detailed information regarding the libraries of the Umayyad, Abbasid, Fatimid, and Muslim Spanish empires.

Nasr, Seyyed Hossein
Science and Civilization in Islam
Cambridge, U.K.: Islamic Texts Society, 1987.
230pp. ISBN: 0-946621-11-X

Explores the theological and philosophical bases for scientific inquiry. Also provides a good introduction into the role of Muslim scientists in the development of world civilization.

Qadir, C.A.
Philosophy and Science in the Islamic World
London: Routledge Inc., 1988.
218pp. ISBN: 0-415-00294-X

A useful resource which discusses the Islamic theory of knowledge and how it applies to scientific inquiry. Provides insights into historical and contemporary viewpoints.

Rosenthal, Franz
The Classical Heritage in Islam
London: Routledge Inc., 1975.
298pp. ISBN: 0-415-07693-5

Explore the interconnections between the classical world of the Greeks and the civilization engendered by Islam. Useful for tracing the development of knowledge and technological progress from ancient times to the present.

Turner, Howard R.
Science in Medieval Islam
Austin: University of Texas Press, 1995.
262pp. ISBN: 0-292-78147-4

A well-structured introduction to the various realms of scientific activity engaged in by Muslims and others. Contains many useful photographs.

Art and Architecture

Brend, Barbara
Islamic Art
1997. 240pp. $26.95

From the Alhambra to the Dome of the Rock, with over 100 color illustrations, this book traces the development of classic Islamic art from the 7th century to the present. Available from Astrolabe.

El-Said, Issam and Ayse Parman
Geometric Concepts in Islamic Art
Palo Alto, CA: Dale Seymour Publications, 1976. 154pp. ISBN: 0-86651-421-X

An excellent source for patterns used in Islamic art and architecture. Contains line-drawings illustrating various geometric concepts as well as photographs of actual historical works.

Friedlander, Shems
Ninety-Nine Names of Allah
San Francisco: HarperCollins, 1993.
128pp. ISBN: 0-06-063034-5

A wonderful pocket-book sized work, containing the meanings of the "Ninety-nine Names" of God mentioned in the Qur'an and Hadith. Each Arabic word is written in a beautiful calligraphic style with the meaning provided below the design.

Ghazi, Bushra Y.
Art of Arabic Calligraphy
Chicago: Iqra Intl. Educational Foundation, 1993. Six volumes. ISBN: 2-221-01101-5

For those interested in the techniques of Arabic calligraphy, this series provides numerous examples and hands-on technical training. Great for art classes.

Nasr, Seyyed Hossein
Islamic Art and Spirituality
New York: State University of New York, 1987.
213pp. ISBN: 0-88706-175-3

A thought-provoking introduction to the relationship between Muslim belief and artistic expression. Issues such as non-representational art, calligraphy, and geometric symbolism are explored.

Numachi, Ali and Seyyed H. Nasr
Mecca the Blessed, Medina the Radiant
1997. 240pp. $49.95

An unprecedented exploration of the two holiest cities in Islam. With nearly 200 pages of stunning photographs. Available from Astrolabe.

Otto-Dorn, Katharina
Art and Architecture of the Islamic World
1991. Library of Congress No. 04325-1

This reference work surveys the unique artistic achievements of Muslim civilization since the advent of Islam. The role of spirituality in the creative process receives special attention.

Rice, David T.
Islamic Art
London: Thames and Hudson Ltd., 1975.
288pp. ISBN: 0-500-20150-1

Excellent overview of various styles and periods of Muslim art, including Abbasid, Spanish, Persian, Mongol, and Ottoman. Concise yet comprehensive.

Safadi, Yasin Hamid
Islamic Calligraphy
London: Thames and Hudson Ltd., 1978.
144pp. ISBN: 0-500-27117-8 $14.95

This beautiful reference work explores Muslim civilization's emphasis on revering the Qur'an through the art of calligraphy. Provides readers with a comprehensive guide to the subject from centuries past to modern-day calligraphic forms. Contains over 200 illustrations.

Seymour, Dale and Jill Barton
Introduction to Tessalations
Palo Alto, CA: Dale Seymour Publications, 1989. 264pp. $19.95

This book explores tessalations, geometric patterns that repeat when individual units are placed across a surface. Learn how to create various patterns found in Islamic art and architecture.

Interreligious Studies

Al-Faruqi, Ismail
Trialogue of the Abrahamic Faiths
Chicago: Kazi Publications, 1986.
88pp. ISBN: 0-912463-06-6

Includes chapters written by Jewish, Christian, and Muslim scholars. Provides valuable insight into the similarities and differences between these three Abrahamic faiths.

Hick, John and Edmund Meltzer, eds.
Three Faiths - One God:
A Jewish, Christian, Muslim Encounter
New York: State University of New York Press, 1989. 240pp. ISBN: 0-7914-0043-3

Explore the interconnections between the three Abrahamic faiths. A useful work containing diverse viewpoints.

Peters, F.E.
Judaism, Christianity, and Islam
1990. ISBN: 0-691-02044-2

Takes the basic texts of the three monotheistic faiths and juxtaposes extensive passages from them to show the similarities and common issues facing the followers of each.

Periodicals

Educators can contact the Council on Islamic Education for copies of selected issues of the following periodicals:

ARAMCO World

Box 3725
Escondido, CA 92033-3725

An excellent source of information about Muslims throughout the world, as well as Muslim art, architecture, etc. Full of beautiful photographs and illustrations. Can be obtained free from ARAMCO.

Islamic Horizons

Islamic Society of North America
P.O. Box 38
Plainfield, IN 46168
(317) 839-8157 ext.235

A high-quality magazine that deals with contemporary topics related to Muslims and Islam in the United States.

The Message

Islamic Circle of North America
166-26 89th Avenue
Jamaica, NY 11432
(718) 658-5163

A monthly magazine covering a wide range of topics, including news on international events, domestic concerns, and Muslim viewpoints on numerous important issues.

The Minaret

Multivera International
434 S. Vermont Avenue
Los Angeles, CA 90020
(213) 384-4570

A well-produced monthly magazine that covers a wide range of contemporary topics related to Islam and Muslims in the United States.

TEACHING RESOURCES

Curricula and Lesson Plans

Brine, Alan
Islam
London: Longman Group, 1991. 64pp.

This book focuses on the cultural ideas and experiences inherent in the Muslim way of life. Contains lesson plan ideas and activities which promote high thinking level skill development.

Images of Conflict—Learning From Media Coverage of the Gulf War

A Media Literacy Workshop Kit
Los Angeles, CA: Center for Media and Values, 1991. $34.95.
ISBN: 1-879419-04-1

A useful tool for teaching media awareness and literacy using the coverage of the Gulf War as a case study. Materials are well-arranged and easy to implement.

MacDonald, Fiona
The World of Islam Up to 1500
New York: HarperCollins, 1991. 64pp.

A lively and comprehensive unit on Muslim history, containing numerous primary and secondary source documents. Provides many activity suggestions for engaging lessons on this vast subject. Units are divided as follows: Muhammad's World, The Spread of Islam, Two Great Cities, Arts and Sciences, and Islam and Other Cultures.

Reese, Lyn
Women of the Muslim Middle Ages
Women of the World, 1992. 83pp.

This curriculum unit, built around two original stories, contains curriculum tie-ins, a student-teacher background essay, vocabulary definitions, activities and worksheets. Unit One explores the life of Queen Amina, a Muslim ruler of an African city-state, while Unit Two contains the story of Kybele, a woman in the Ottoman Turkish court of Suleyman the Magnificent.

Shabbas, Audrey, ed.
A Medieval Banquet in the Alhambra Palace
Berkeley: Arab World And Islamic Resources (AWAIR), 1992. 176pp. $29.95

Students recreate a feast in Muslim Spain, at the famed Alhambra. Curriculum unit contains overviews of Muslim contributions to science and explores Muslim culture and society during Europe's "medieval" period. Ancillary items such as slides and music audio cassette also available.

Siddiqui, Zeba
Karavan: Tales and Plays for Children
Plainfield, IN: American Trust Publications, 1990. 141pp. ISBN: 0-8925-9-088-2

A collection of plays with lessons about the beliefs and principles of Islam and Muslims. JH/HS

Student Reading and Activities

Alexander, Sue
Nadia The Willful
New York: Pantheon Books, 1983. 44pp. ISBN: 0-394-85265-6

An endearing story about a strong-willed girl, and the valuable lesson she provides for her family after a crisis takes place. Recommended. Elem./Jr. High

Al-Jabarti, Abd al-Rahman. Shmuel Moreh, tr.
Napolean in Egypt - Al-Jabarti's Chronicle of the First Seven Months of French Occupation, 1798
New York: Markus Wiener Publishing, 1993. 185pp. ISBN: 1-55876-070-9

Interesting account by one of Egypt's most prominent writers and historians of the time. Also includes French viewpoint written by Napolean's private secretary, and an essay on Orientalism by renowned scholar Edward Said.

Alshalabi, Firyal
Ahmed's Alphabet Book

Young Ahmed tells about himself and his family.

Ara, Zeenat and Zeba Siddiqui
Muslim World Coloring Book
Plainfield, IN: American Trust Publications, 1987. 30pp.

Contains scenes from around the Muslim world, ready for coloring. Great for kindergarten and elementary-level students. K-3.

Asad, Mohammad
The Road to Mecca
Gibraltar, Spain: Dar al-Andalus, 1980. 380pp.

A fascinating account of one of the most renowned thinkers of the modern era, the late Muhammad Asad. Journey with him as he retraces his experiences in the Middle East during the earlier part of this century. JH./HS

As-Saffar, Muhammad. S.G. Miller, tr.
Disorienting Encounters - Travels of a Moroccan Scholar in France (1845-1846)
Berkeley: University of California Press, 1992.

An interesting and sometimes humorous account of 17th century France, from the standpoint of a foreign visitor. Excellent source for engaging multicultural and historical reading. JH/HS

Azrak, Michel and M.J.L. Young, eds.
Modern Syrian Short Stories
Three Continents Press, 1988. 180pp.

Contains 18 diverse short stories by 18 different authors. Helps provide English-language readers broaden their awareness of life and culture in Syria. HS

Bahous, Sally
Sitti and the Cats: A Tale of Friendship

From the oral tradition of Palestine, an old woman rescues a kitten and is rewarded for her generosity.

Balit, Christina
Arabian Home: Leila and Mustapha's Story
Hampstead Press, 1988.
ISBN: 0-531-19506-6

An interesting story about two young children growing up in Saudi Arabia. Elem./Jr. High

Barboza, Steven
American Jihad - Islam After Malcolm X
New York: Doubleday, 1993.
370pp. ISBN: 0-385-47011-8

A collection of personal interviews collected from a diverse set of American Muslims. Learn about the fascinating experiences of immigrants, native-born Muslims, and converts to Islam. JH/HS

Bennis, Phyllis and Michel Moushabeck, eds.
Beyond the Storm - A Gulf Crisis Reader
Interlink Publishing, 1991. 412pp. $14.95

With a forward by Edward Said, this anthology contains writings and contributions from more than 30 writers, analysts, scholars, poets and activists. An important resource for teachers interested in preparing a balanced survey of the Gulf crisis. HS

Burgoyne, Diane T.
Amina and Muhammad's Special Visitor
Middle East Gateway Series, 1982.
58pp. Library of Congress No. 82-90927

A well-written and enjoyable story about two young children in Arabia, and the fun they have when their uncle from America visits. K-3.

Bushnaq, Inea, tr.
Arab Folktales
New York: Pantheon Books, 1986.
386pp. ISBN: 0-394-75179-5

A compilation of folktales and stories from various Arab countries. Highly entertaining. Elem./Jr. High/HS

Chaudhry, Saida
Call to Prophethood
Plainfield, IN: American Trust Publications, 1983. 16pp. ISBN: 0-89259-046-7

Students learn about the Muslim view of prophethood and the role of Muhammad as the final prophet. Narrates in a simple language Muhammad's life from childhood to the time of the first revelations of the Qur'an. Elem./Jr. High

Dunn, Ross E.
The Adventures of Ibn Battuta
Berkeley: University of California Press, 1986.
357pp. ISBN: 0-520-06743-6

Anyone interested in what life was like in the 14th century will find this book interesting. Ibn Battuta was a Muslim who traveled over 75,000 miles for 28 years, and documented the many wonders he encountered throughout the Old World. HS

Durkee, Noura
The Amazing Adventures of Ibn Battuta

An excellent, colorful book about one of the most famous travelers that ever lived. Ideal for younger students. Available from Astrolabe. Elem./Jr. High

Easwaran, Eknath
A Man to Match His Mountains: Badshah Khan, Nonviolent Soldier of Islam
Petaluma, CA: Nilgiri Press, 1985. 240pp.

This is the story of Badsha Khan, a Muslim leader who led a group of nonviolent followers in resisting British rule in India. He was, according to Gandhi, "the real father of nonviolence." An important work which challenges the myth of Islam as a violent religion. HS

El-Moslimany, Ann P.
Zaki's Ramadan Fast
Seattle: Amica Publishing House, 1994.
32pp. ISBN: 1-884187-08-0

A wonderful story about a young boy's day during Ramadan. Nicely-illustrated. Highly recommended for raising young students' awareness of the Muslim lifestyle. Elem./Jr. High

Emerick, Yahiya
What Islam Is All About
New York: IBTS, 1997. 420pp.

A textbook of Islamic Studies patterned after modern textbook styles, suited to Muslim students and adult learners Contains teacher's guide and enrichment literature. JH/HS

Ghazi, Abidullah
Grandfather's Orchard
Seattle: Amica International, 1993.
24pp. ISBN: 1-56316-307-1

A beautiful story about tradition and love within a Muslim family. Grandfather explains that planting an orchard is a way of passing on love from generation to generation. Highly recommended. Elem./Jr. High

Ghazi, Rashid
The World of Islam Coloring Book
Chicago: Kazi Publications, 1982.
42pp. ISBN: 0-395782-08-7

Coloring book containing flags of Muslim countries. Also provides population, language, and geographical information. Elem./Jr. High

Ghazi, Suhaib Hamid
Ramadan
New York: Holiday House, 1996.
ISBN: 0-8234-1275-X

An excellent children's book on the Muslim month of fasting. Winner of a book award from the National Council for the Social Studies. Elem./Jr. High

Heide, Florence and Judith Gilliland
The Day of Ahmed's Secret
New York: Lothrop, Lee & Shepard Books, 1990. 32pp.

A simple yet interesting tale of a young boy's hard work and first big accomplishment. Illustrated in water-color style. Elem./Jr. High

Heide, Florence and Judith Gilliland
The House of Wisdom

Tells the story of Ishaq bin Hunayn and the House of Wisdom, Baghdad's 9th-century library and translation center.

Husain, Sharukh
What Do We Know About Islam
48pp.

A very colorful large-format introductory book ideal for grades 2 through 5 An excellent resource for lower grades as well as middle school. Available from Astrolabe. Elem./Jr. High

Hutchinson, Haji Uthman
Invincible Abdullah: The Deadly Mountain Revenge
Plainfield, IN: American Trust Publications. 220pp. ISBN: 0-89259-121-8
Invincible Abdullah: The Car Theft Kidnapping
Plainfield, IN: American Trust Publ. 152pp.
Invincible Abdullah: The Mystery of the Missing Pearls
Plainfield, IN: American Trust Publ. 131pp.
Invincible Abdullah: The Wilderness Survival
Plainfield, IN: American Trust Publ. 131pp.

This series of books is written in the Hardy Boys tradition, with high adventure for Abdullah and his friends around every corner. Very entertaining. Jr. High

Ibn Jubayr. Ronald J.C. Broadhurst, tr.
The Travels of Ibn Jubayr
London: Jonathan Cape, 1952.

An intriguing account by a famous Muslim traveler. A good addition to material on renowned world traveler Ibn Battuta. JH/HS

Id-ul-Fitr
32pp.

This book highlights the joyous celebration called Id ul-Fitr that ends Ramadan, and describes special prayers, festivities and family gatherings related to the Muslim holiday. Available from Astrolabe. Elem./Jr. High

Irving, Thomas B.
Falcon of Spain
Lahore, Pakistan: Muhammad Ashraf, 1980.

Engaging narrative that tells the story of Abd al-Rahman I, who in 756 C.E. became the first Umayyad ruler of Muslim Spain. Helps students learn about an aspect of European history seldom explored in depth. HS

Johnson-Davies, Denys
Folktales of Egypt
Hoopoe Books, 1993. 48pp.

Seven rich and imaginative stories adapted from Egyptian oral tradition. Very enjoyable. JH/HS

Johnson-Davies, Denys
Stories of the Caliphs: Early Rulers of Islam

This book contains twenty-seven historically based stories from the lives of the early rulers of the Muslim community. Illustrated. Available from Astrolabe. Elem./Jr. High

Kayani, M. Salim
Assalamu Alaikum
Leicester, U.K.: Islamic Foundation, 1993. 26pp. ISBN: 0-86037-076-3

A nice book for elementary-level students. Emphasizes the importance of peace in the lives of Muslims, exemplified by the traditional greeting. K-3

Kazemi, Reza Shah
Avicenna

Known as Ibn Sina, he was considered the "prince of physicians." Students learn about one of the most famous doctors in world history. Available from Astrolabe. Elem./Jr. High

Kezzeiz, Ediba
Grandma's Garden
Plainfield, IN: American Trust Publications, 1991. 21pp.

An interesting story emphasizing human responsibility as caretakers of the earth and stresses thanking God for His bounty. Elem./Jr. High

Kezzeiz, Ediba
The Ramadan Adventures of Fasfoose Mouse
Plainfield, IN: American Trust Publications, 1991. 44pp.

This delightful tale, in which Jamilah, a young American Muslim girl, befriends a family of mice, explores the circumstances surrounding the month of fasting, Ramadan. Elem./Jr. High

Khalidi, Marion
Saladin

Salah al-Din (Saladin) was one of the most famous Muslim leaders in history. Learn about his impressive character and his success against the Crusaders. Available from Astrolabe. Elem./Jr. High

Khan, Rukhsana
Muslim Child
Napoleon Publishing, 1999.
ISBN: 0-929141-61-X

A collection of short stories and poems that deals with the everyday life of Muslim children. Each story illustrates a major tenet of Islam. Using non-fiction sidebars and quotations from Islam's religious scriptures, this book provides a comprehensive overview of Islam. JH/HS

Dahling if You Luv Me Would You Please Please Smile
ISBN: 0-7737-6016-4

The Roses in My Carpets
ISBN: 0-7737-3092-3
Other wonderful books with Islamic themes by the same author.

Khan, S. Azmath Ali
Islamic Architecture Coloring Book
Chicago: Iqra Intl. Educational Foundation, 1992. 28pp.

Teach students about important Islamic monuments and structures through coloring. Ideal for elementary grade levels. Elem./Jr. High

Khattab, Huda
Stories from the Muslim World
Morristown, NJ: Silver Burdett Press, 1990. 43pp. ISBN: 0-382-09313-5

An excellent work containing several stories about well-known and popular Muslim figures in history. Beautifully illustrated. Elem./Jr. High

Kilani, Rasheed and Ambara
Kitabi
Milestone Publications, 1992. 124pp.

This one-of-a-kind, nicely-illustrated book comes with an audio-cassette to help children learn the Arabic alphabet. Contains practice drills, assignments and games as well. Highly recommended as an introduction to the language. Elem./Jr. High

Knight, Khadija
World Religions: Islam
48pp.

An excellent introductory survey text for middle school students. Covers Muslim beliefs, practices and history. Available from Astrolabe. Elem./Jr. High

Lockman, Zachary and Joel Beinin, eds.
Intifada - The Palestinian Uprising Against Israeli Occupation
Boston: South End Press, 1989. 423pp.

Prepared by two Jewish members of the editorial board of the Middle East Research and Information Project (MERIP), this resource contains eye-witness accounts, poetry and primary source documents from numerous contributors. An important tool for teachers wanting to provide a balanced approach to this difficult subject. HS

Maalouf, Amin
Leo The African
London: Quartet Books Ltd., 1986. 360pp. ISBN: 0-7043-2613-2

A fictionalized account of the historical figure Hasan al-Wazan, also known as Leo Africanus. After the fall of Muslim Spain in 1492, Hasan sets out on a journey that lasts a lifetime. Highly readable. JH/HS

MacDonald, Fiona and Mark Bergin
A 16th Century Mosque
New York: Peter Bedrick Books, 1994. 48pp. ISBN: 0-87226-310-X

A beautifully illustrated book containing detailed drawings and descriptions of features of the 16th century mosque, which historically served as a focal point for the Muslim community. Highly-recommended. Elem./Jr. High

MacDonald, Fiona and Joan Ullathorne
Ibn Tulun: Story of a Mosque
37pp.

A beautifully illustrated book which tells the story of one of the oldest and most famous mosques, built by the great leader Ahmad Ibn Tulun. Contains a comprehensive glossary. Elem./Jr. High

MacMillan, Diane M.
Ramadan and Id al-Fitr
Hillsdale, NJ: Enslow Publishers, 1994. 48pp. ISBN: 0-89490-502-3

A good introduction to Islam for younger readers. Emphasizes the Muslim fasting month and the holiday which follows. Contains many interesting photographs. Elem./Jr. High

Marshall, Julia
Cheng Ho

This famous Muslim admiral served under the Ming dynasty in China. Learn about his extensive sea travels in the Far East. Available from Astrolabe. Elem./Jr. High

McDermott, Mustafa Y.
Muslim Nursery Rhymes
Leicester, U.K.: The Islamic Foundation, 1989. 40pp.

Sixteen nursery rhymes for pre-school and kindergarten students, illustrated in full color. A useful resource for Muslim parents as well. K-3

Matthews, Mary
Magid Fasts for Ramadan
48pp.

A charming story about a boy who is convinced he is old enough to fast, though his parents and older siblings don't think so. The story, set in modern-day Egypt, recounts Magid's struggle and its happy resolution, and in the process, gives readers a better understanding of Islamic beliefs and practices. Available from Astrolabe. Elem./Jr. High

Murad, Khurram and M. Salim Kayani
The Kingdom of Justice
Leicester, U.K.: The Islamic Foundation. 48pp.

Seven stories, based on historical accounts, of Muslim society during the leadership of the second Caliph, Umar ibn al-Khattab. Helps teachers explore Islamic values and important concepts of law and justice found in Islam. Comes with lively and engaging narrative audio-cassette. Elem./Jr. High

Murad, Khurram and M. Salim Kayani

The Longing Heart

Leicester, U.K.: The Islamic Foundation. 28pp.

This historically-based story tells of Abu Dhar, the leader of a Bedouin tribe, who seeks out Prophet Muhammad after hearing of him, and who subsequently becomes one of Muhammad's closest companions. Comes with lively and engaging narrative audio-cassette. Elem./Jr. High

Murad, Khurram

Stories of the Caliphs

Leicester, U.K.: The Islamic Foundation. 48pp.

Six stories, based on historical accounts, of Muslim society during the leadership of the four "Rightly Guided" Caliphs, Abu Bakr, Umar, Uthman and Ali. Helps teachers explore Islamic values and ethics, and the Islamic concept of leadership. Comes with lively and engaging narrative audio-cassette. Elem./Jr. High

Murad, Khurram

The Wise Poet

Leicester, U.K.: The Islamic Foundation, 1985. 26pp. ISBN: 0-86037-150-6

This historically-based story, set during the time of Prophet Muhammad, tells of a renowned poet's interactions with the Quraysh tribe, who tried to dissuade him from listening to the Prophet. Comes with lively and engaging narrative audio-cassette. Elem./Jr. High

The Prophets

Chicago: Iqra Intl. Educational Foundation, 1993. 47pp.

A wonderfully water-color illustrated storybook, with accounts of four great prophets: Abraham, Moses, Jesus, and Muhammad. Highly recommended. Elem./Jr. High

Qazi, M.A.

Arabic Alphabets Coloring Book

Chicago: Kazi Publications, 1984. 32pp.

Help students learn the strokes and angles of individual Arabic letters. Ideal for elementary grade levels. K-6

Rummel, Jack

Malcolm X

New York: Chelsea House, 1989. 110pp. ISBN: 1-55546-600-1

An excellent biography of this important figure, ideally suited for younger readers. Contains many illustrations and photographs. JH

Rummel, Jack

Muhammad Ali

New York: Chelsea House, 1988. 126pp.

An interesting and well-written biography of one of boxing's greatest legends. Contains many illustrations and photographs. JH

Shah, Amina

The Tale of the Four Dervishes and Other Sufi Tales

San Francisco: Harper & Row, 1981. 259pp. ISBN: 0-06-067256-0

Enchanting, good-humored tales set in the time of Muslim civilization's prominence. A good alternative to "A Thousand and One Nights." JH/HS

Shah, Idries and Safia

Afghan Caravan

Octagon Press, 1991. 336pp.

A collection of writings narrating the unique stories of a Pathan princess and other characters. Contains many jokes, recipes and other tidbits throughout. Students learn about the Afghani Muslim culture through this rich and valuable resource. JH/HS

Sharif, Zeenat

Zeenat's All About Prayer Rugs Coloring Book

Plainfield, IN: American Trust Publications, 1986. 25pp.

Coloring book emphasizing various patterns and designs of Muslim prayer rugs. Also includes instructions for a student prayer rug design project. K-6

Siddiqui, Abia

Mosques of the World Coloring Book

London: TaHa Publications, 1983. 16pp.

Arts of the Muslim World Coloring Book

London: TaHa Publications, 1983. 19pp.

Help students learn about cultural diversity in Islam through various mosque structures around the world, and give students a feeling for the Islamic artistic tradition. Ideal for elementary grade levels. K-6

Siddiqui, Zeba

Kareem and Fatima

Plainfield, IN: American Trust Publications, 1990. 152pp. ISBN: 0-89259-009-2

A well-written storybook about a Muslim family. Ideal for middle-school level students. Elem./Jr. High

Stanley, Diane

Fortune

New York: Morrow Junior Books, 1990. ISBN: 0-688-07210-0

A beautifully-illustrated and enchanting story that is sure to please children everywhere. The story involves princes, princesses, and a magic tiger. The illustrations are in a style reminiscent of Persian Muslim art. Excellent. Elem./Jr. High

Tahan, Malba

The Man Who Counted - A Collection of Mathematical Adventures

W.W. Norton, 1993. ISBN: 0-393-30934-7

A series of problem-solving and mathematical adventures framed around the travels of Beremiz Samir during the 10th century. His mathematical genius enables him to settle disputes, overcome danger, and gain fame and fortune. An excellent resource. JH/HS

Tergeman, Siham

Daughter of Damascus

Austin: University of Texas Press, 1994. 202pp.

A memoir of life as a Syrian Muslim woman living in the early twentieth century. An engaging piece of literature which gives an insider's view of Syrian Muslim society. HS

Travelers and Explorers

Chicago: Iqra Intl. Educational Foundation, 1993. 47pp.

Beautifully-illustrated storybook about various Muslim travelers and explorers who lived in the "Middle Ages." A must-have. Elem./Jr. High

Wolfe, Michael

The Hadj

331pp. $21.95

The author, an ABC news correspondent and an American Muslim, narrates his travels throughout North Africa and in Makkah. Available from Astrolabe. JH/HS

Wolfe, Michael

One Thousand Roads to Mecca

620pp. $32.50

A unique compilation of texts by observant writers from the East and West over the last ten centuries, converging on Mecca. Available from Astrolabe. JH/HS

Wormser, Richard

American Islam: Growing Up Muslim in America

130pp.

An engaging book in which young Muslims speak about every day concerns—family, school, relationships— and the challenges of practicing their faith. Available from Astrolabe. JH/HS

Manipulatives

Arabic Alphabet Poster

Based on an original poster published in Egypt, it features the same captivating illustrations by a renowned Egyptian artist. The poster also provides an Arabic-English glossary of the images depicted. Available in paper ($10) and laminated ($15) editions. Dimensions are 22" by 34". A four-page "Guide to the Arabic Language" is also included. Available from AMIDEAST.

Arabic Letter Playing Cards

Set of playing cards marked with the letters of the Arabic alphabet. Use them as flashcards or for card games. Two styles. Ideal for kindergarten and elementary school students. Available for $4.00 per set from Iqra Intl. Book Center.

Calligraphy Notecards

Printed in black and gold, these cards contain Arabic proverbs in a classical calligraphic style. Set of ten cards, two each of five designs, for $12 plus postage and handling. Available from AMIDEAST.

Middle East and North Africa Map

This large, affordable map depicts the Middle East and Africa, giving a much broader view of the geographic center of the Muslim world. Major cities, water bodies, mountain ranges, and deserts are labeled. Surrounding areas in Africa, Asia, and Europe are lightly shaded to provide geographical context. Paper edition is $10, plus postage and handling. The laminated version ($20 plus p/h) can be written on with a dry marker and wiped clean. Comes complete with grommets for easy display. Dimensions are 57" by 37". Also includes blackline master showing outlines only. Available from AMIDEAST.

Model Quadrant

The Muslims invented it, Columbus used it, and now your students can combine the study of history, astronomy, and math as they learn to find their latitude using this model quadrant. Printed on heavy board and varnished to minimize wear and tear from many hands, the quadrant comes complete with illustrated step-by-step instructions for use, a table of solar declinations, and discussion questions. Available from AMIDEAST for $6.95 plus postage and handling.

Muslim Clothing

For classroom presentations and activities, these articles of clothing from several Muslim cultures are ideal. Items include traditional Arab kuffiyeh (checkered headcloth), kufi (cap worn in many Asian Muslim cultures), and women's headcovering in various colors and patterns.

Prayer Rug

Useful for studying about the form and function of Muslim worship. Comes with small booklet describing the worship positions and prayers involved.

Yearly Calendars

Produced annually with both Gregorian and Islamic Hijri dates. Calendars with useful facts, figures, and original illustrations and designs by Muslim artists are available from AMICA International (Seattle, WA) and the Islamic Society of North America (Plainfield, IN).

VIDEO AND AUDIO RESOURCES

ABC News Nightline — The Hajj (4/18/97)

1997. ABC News. Available from Astrolabe Pictures.

An excellent video which follows the journey of American Muslim Michael Wolfe, ABC News correspondent, as he performs the pilgrimage to Makkah. Get an insider's view of this unique spiritual event which every Muslim longs to experience.

al-Andalus - The Heritage of Islamic Spain

1992. Sociedad Estatal Quinto Centario, Madrid, Spain. 57 min.

This film focuses on the treasures of Islamic Spain exhibited in Granada and at the Metropolitan Museum, New York in 1992, commemorating 1492. Excellent visuals.

Art and the Islamic World

1993. Middle East Institute. 33 min.

Excellent film providing insight into the multivaried Islamic artistic tradition. Images of calligraphy, ceramics, masjid architecture, miniature paintings, scientific drawings, carpets and metalwork. Highly recommended.

Best Women Reciters of the Qur'an

1993. Available from Sound Vision. 29 min.

This special album of two audio-cassettes contains Qur'anic recitation from two of the world's best women reciters. Refreshing and inspiring.

Bosnia - The Untold Story

1993. Available from Sound Vision.

Provides a glimpse into the tragic plight of the Bosnian Muslims. Delves into the history of the region, and contains testimonials from victims of the genocide.

Frontline: Muslims

2002. Independent Production Fund. Available from www.mysticfire.com.

Takes an in-depth look at what it means to be a Muslim in the 21st century. Filmed in Egypt, Malaysia, Iran, Turkey, Nigeria and the U.S., the video explores the influence of culture and politics on religion, and provides a deeper understanding of the political forces at work among Muslims around the world.

Islam - A Closer Look

1995. Taibah Intl. Aid Association.

Well known Muslim personalities and scholars of Islam share their insights regarding the faith and its adherents.

Islam - A Pictorial Essay

Islamic Texts Society.

A colorful, well produced video which helps elaborate the broad outlines of Islam as a faith and as a foundation for Muslim civilization.

Islam in America

Producer: Lindsay Miller
1992. Christian Science Monitor Video.

A highly recommended production that provides insight into the history of Islam in America, as well as a glimpse into the lives of several Muslim Americans living throughout the country.

Islamic Views on Terrorism, Jihad, and Human Rights

1986. Available from Kazi Publications.

Videotape of a lecture by Professor Jamal Badawi delivered at the University of Kansas in Lawrence, KS.

Living Islam

1993. Produced by the British Broadcasting Corporation. Available from Ambrose Video. Six parts.

A six-part journey into the diverse world of Muslim faith and practice. Contains glimpses of life in nineteen different countries, as well as interviews with leading Muslim scholars. This film was initiated by renowned Muslim scholar Akbar S. Ahmed.

Malcolm X

Director: Spike Lee
1992. Warner Brothers.

This film explores the many transitions that characterized the life of El-Hajj Malik El-Shabazz, popularly known as Malcolm X. Some beautiful scenes of the Hajj make an exceptionally good teaching tool. Can be obtained from most video rental stores.

Men and Women's Relations in Islam

1988. Available from Kazi Publications.

Videotape of a two-hour presentation given by Professor Jeffery Lang in Lawrence, Kansas in 1988 at the University of Kansas.

The Message

Director: Mustapha Akkad
Available from Sound Vision. 197 min.

An epic production in the vein of "The Ten Commandments," starring Anthony Quinn and Irene Papas. Provides students with a cohesive understanding of the events surrounding Muhammad's call to prophethood and his subsequent mission.

Muhammad Ali: In His Own Words

Available from Astrolabe. $19.95
Contains footage discussing Ali's refusal to join the U.S. Army on religious grounds and his many humanitarian efforts around the world. 40 min.

Qur'an on CD

1994. Available from Sound Vision.

Complete Qur'an on 25 CDs recited by famous Qari Shaykh Abdul Basit. Each chapter of the Qur'an is an independent track for easy access.

Ramadan

1997. Available from Astrolabe.

This interactive children's educational video explores the meaning and explains the various rituals of Ramadan. Ideal for grades K through 4. 25 min. Available from Astrolabe.

The Speeches of Malcolm X

Available from Astrolabe. $19.95

Rare footage shows the evolution of Malcolm X's beliefs. Includes discussion with Mike Wallace of CBS News. 41 min. Available from Astrolabe.

Topkapi Palace

1992. MTV, Inc., Turkey. Seven part series.

This film series examines the whole Topkapi palace complex, from which twenty-four Ottoman sultans ruled. Miniatures, engravings and other illustrations are included.

Women's Rights and Roles in Islam

1994. Available from Sound Vision.

A debate about women in Islam between a journalist writing for a major city newspaper and a noted Muslim woman writer and activist. Thought-provoking and sure to stimulate further discussion.

The Wonders of Islamic Science

1994. Available from Sound Vision.

This fascinating documentary describes the achievements of Muslims in astronomy, medicine, mathematics, geography, botany, and other fields. Provides insight into the role of the Qur'an in inspiring these efforts.

Word Power in Islamic Art

1992. Media Center, University of Toronto. 12 min.

This brief film focuses on how writing became a form of decoration in Islamic art. Includes outstanding oud music.

COMPUTER RESOURCES

Qur'an, Hadith, and Shari'ah

The Alim 3.0 - An Islamic study toolkit which includes Qur'an in Arabic and English translations, commentaries on the *Qur'an*, *Sahih Bukhari Hadith*, Islamic Subjects database, dictionary of terms.
Requires: PC-compatible, DOS, 512K RAM, 1.5-15 MB free on hard drive, EGA or better display.
Price: $115
Available: ISL Software Corp. (800) 397-5561 or (512) 690-5973.

Al-Hadith Database- Contains the following collections of hadith in English: *Sahih Bukhari, Sahih Muslim, Abu Dawud, Al-Muwatta,Tirmidhi,* and *Nasa'i.* This program cross-references with Al-Qur'anBase.
Requires: PC-compatible, DOS, 512K RAM, 20 MB free on hard drive (also available for Windows).
Price: $79
Available: MVI Bookstore, 434 S. Vermont Ave., Los Angeles, CA 90020. (213) 384-4570.

Hadith on CD - Collections of *hadith* databases on CD ROM. Over 15 languages supported.
Requires: PC-compatible with CD ROM drive.
Available: Center for Hadith Analysis, 805 29th St. #552-N, Boulder, CO 80303. (303) 938-1211.

HadithBase - Contains all nine volumes of *Sahih Bukhari*, a collection of the most authentic sayings of Prophet Muhammad. Extensive search capabilities.
Requires: PC compatible, DOS, 512K RAM, 5 MB free on hard drive.
Price: $59
Available: Sound Vision.

Islamic LawBase - A program that enables users to search the following legal sources in English: *Fiqh as-Sunnah, Majellah al-Ahkam, Hedaya al-Marghinani, Fatawa-e-Qazi Azam, Al Halal Wal Haram, Muwatta, al Risala al-Qairawaniya, Criminal Law of Islam.*
Requires: PC-compatible, DOS, 512K RAM, 20 MB free on hard drive.
Price: $199
Available: MVI Bookstore, 434 S. Vermont Ave., Los Angeles, CA 90020. (213) 384-4570.

Al-Qari - Unique program that teaches users how to read, spell, and recite *Qur'anic* Arabic. Combines sound, graphics, text and animation to provide a user-friendly, stimulating learning experience.
Requires: PC-compatible: 4MB RAM, 20 MB free on hard drive, Sound Blaster; Macintosh: System 6.0.5 or higher, 2.8 MB RAM, 16 MB free on hard drive.
Price: $129
Available: Sound Vision.

Al-Quran Database - *Qur'anic* text with English translation by A. Yusuf Ali and M. Pickthall. Searchable English text by keyword and subject. Complements Al-Hadith Database.
Requires: PC-compatible, DOS, 512K RAM, 10 MB free (also available for Windows).
Price: $79
Available: MVI Bookstore, 434 S. Vermont Ave., Los Angeles, CA 90020. (213) 384-4570.

Qur'an on Mac - *Qur'anic* text with English translation by A. Yusuf Ali.
Requires: Macintosh, System 7.0.
Price: $145
Available: General Trade and Technology, 4505 Allstate Dr. #108, Riverside, CA 92501. (909) 788-8729.

Qur'anBase - Research tool for English translation of the *Qur'an.* Extensive search capabilities.
Requires: PC-compatible, DOS, 256K RAM, 1.5 MB free on hard drive; Macintosh, System 6.0.5 or higher, 1.5 MB free on hard drive.
Price: $49
Available: Sound Vision.

Quiz Programs

Al Hadi 1.0 - Contains questions on pillars of Islam, prayers, Ramadan, terminology, etc.
Requires: PC-compatible, Windows, 2MB RAM; Macintosh, System 7.0 or higher, Hypercard 2.0, 2 MB RAM.
Available: Afrisoft Ltd., 1815 Wellington Rd., Los Angeles, CA 90019. (213) 731-LINK.

Islamiyat - Quiz program with multiple levels, on topics related to Islam and Muslim history.
Requires: PC-compatible, 128K RAM.
Price: $25
Available: Manar Technologies, 3424 25th Street N.E., Calgary, Alberta Canada TIY 6CI. (403) 250-2333.

pcIQ - Multiple choice quiz game on topics related to Islam and Muslim history. Multiple levels of difficulty.
Requires: IBM PC or compatible, 128K RAM
Price: $49
Available: Sound Vision.

Prayer-time Calculators

An-Nida 2.1 - Calculates prayer time schedules for any month of any year (up to 2050) for any location in the world. Comes preset for more than 550 locations. Many features.
Requires: MAC, System 6.0.5 or higher, Hypercard 2.0
Price: $39
Available: Sound Vision.

Minaret 1.3 - A menu-driven program to calculate prayer times for many cities. Produces text output of prayer schedules.
Requires: MAC, System 6.0.5 or higher.
Price: $10 (shareware)
Available: Kamal Abdali, P.O. Box 65207, Washington, DC 20035.

Clip Art

Arabesque Patterns and Clip Art - One hundred geometric and floral patterns in EPS format.
Requires: MAC, System 6.0.5 or higher, or PC-compatible, and program capable of importing EPS files.
Price: $49.95
Available: Arabesque Software Co., 329 S. Mayfair Ave. Ste. 212, Daly City, CA 94015. (415) 495-8655.

IslamiClip Designs#1 - Thirty calligraphic images in EPS format.
Requires: MAC, System 6.0.5 or higher, or PC-compatible, and program capable of importing EPS files.
Price: $49.00
Available: Sakkal Design, 1523 175th Place SE, Bothell, WA 98012. (206) 484-8830.

Word Processing

Al Kaatib 1.23 - Software that automatically switches at the touch of a button from a left to right orientation and vice-versa, making it easy to produce documents with both Arabic and English text. Useful for high-school and college students.
Requires: MAC, System 7 or higher, or PC-compatible with Windows.
Price: $99
Available: Sound Vision.

MATERIALS NOT RECOMMENDED FOR CLASSROOM USE

The following items are materials which teachers should avoid using as instructional materials, as they violate commonly-held ground rules for teaching about religion, such as those elaborated by the First Amendment Center at Vanderbilt University. Please see the preceding sections for a variety of alternative books and videos.

Books

Shabanu: Daughter of the Wind
by Suzanne Fisher Staples (Random House, 1991)

There is a tremendous gap in usable books for the junior high age which focus on young girls. For that reason, many classrooms are turning to the "Shabanu" series, such as *Shabanu, Daughter of the Wind* or *Daughter of the Desert*. These are tales of a young Muslim village girl from Pakistan. There are some good qualities to the books. *Daughter of the Desert*, for instance gives the young reader a graphic understanding of the delicate balance of desert life. For instance, the family faces tremendous perils brought on by a storm. On the other hand, while the character of Shabanu is somewhat "spunky" and independent at times, the main focus of the book is that worn-out "who will I marry" story line which authors use to rope in every adolescent female reader. This continues the stereotype that the only thing on the mind of a young Muslim female is marriage. Shabanu can't marry the boy she "loves" and she rebels against the marriage arranged by her family. The ending of the book is quite unfortunate in that the last scene literally has her father catching up with his run-away daughter and beating her as the book closes!!

Another caution concerning this and any other book about more traditional cultures. At times these books can create a "literary culture class". Modern western societies, particularly in North America, tend to value the individual, putting the independent, "me" before the family, the community, etc. These can clash with the values of those societies which maintain the focus upon what is good for the *group* rather than the individual. It's important to use caution when reading books like *Shabanu, Daughter of the Wind*. It is easy for junior high age students to view parental control over their children as something "bad", and "good old All American rebellion" as something to be placed upon a pedestal. Not only is this blatant ethnocentric thinking, but it can also create real problems for those students in your classroom who are members of a traditional culture and who are trying to maintain a balance between their family's expectations and peer pressures at school.

Videos

Not Without My Daughter

(MGM Productions, 1991)

The screenplay for this film is based on Betty Mahmoody's book by the same name, in which she recounts her experiences as the wife of an Iranian physician who decides to return to Iran shortly following the Iranian revolution in 1979. By mixing cultural, political and religious features of Iranian society, the story does a disservice to viewers' understanding of Islam. In fact, the premise that religion is archaic and backwards is a theme that runs throughout the film. Images of violence, whether domestic or civic, are juxtaposed with shots of worshippers in prayer or engaged in other pious activities. Furthermore, the implication that Western mores and views are superior to those offered by Islam is by no means subtle. Viewers' emotions are manipulated by dialogue which reinforces stereotypes about Islam and Muslims, and by a major plot turn which has Mahmoody almost separated from her daughter Mahtab.

While some educators have used this film to shed light on Iranian and Muslim life, it is an unacceptable teaching tool, which only serves to alienate young Muslim students in the classroom even as it maligns one of the world's major faith traditions. Most importantly, the film falls short as a teaching tool due to its violation of a number of prevailing ground rules for teaching about religion, including the need to avoid reductionism, the necessity of allowing a religion or culture to speak for itself with an authentic voice, and the importance of presenting information in an open-ended manner which avoids perpetuation of foregone conclusions. Clearly, this film was not designed as an instructional piece (despite the inherent didactic ramifications for the general public), and nor should it be used as such in the classroom.

Jihad in America

This purported documentary is in fact nothing less than a carefully crafted propaganda piece designed to instill irrational fears about American Muslims among mainstream viewers. The narrator, Steven Emerson, is a self-identified expert on "Islamic fundamentalism" who in this work patches together unrelated pieces of information and statements by other so-called experts to paint a scenario in which America is in imminent danger from "Islamic radicals." This despite the fact that domestic terrorism is a far more real concern for Americans, as evident from the 1995 bombing in Oklahoma City. Educators must be wary of this film and other materials like it which masquerade as bona fide educational material, but may in fact be a product of those with ulterior or even external interests in perpetuating the notion of an Islamic boogieman. Most importantly, the film's violation of a number of prevailing ground rules for teaching about religion, including the need for fairness and balance as well as showing diversity of opinion within faith traditions, preclude its use in the classroom.

SELECTED PUBLISHERS AND RESOURCE ORGANIZATIONS

Amana Publications
10710 Tucker Street, Suite B
Beltsville, MD 20705
301-595-5777

American Trust Publications (ATP)
2622 E. Main Street
Plainfield, IN 46168
317-839-9278

AMICA Publishing House
1201 First Avenue South, Suite 203
Seattle, WA 98134
206-467-1035

AMIDEAST
1100 17th Street NW
Washington, D.C. 20036-4601
202-785-0022

Arab World and Islamic Resources and School Services (AWAIR)
1865 Euclid Avenue, Suite 4
Berkeley, CA 94709
510-704-0517

Astrolabe Pictures
201 Davis Drive, Suite I
Sterling, VA 20164
800-39-ASTRO
www.astrolabepictures.com

IQRA Intl. Educational Foundation
7450 Skokie Blvd.
Skokie, IL 60077
800-521-4272

Kazi Publications
3023 W. Belmont Avenue
Chicago, IL 60618
773-267-7001   www.kazi.org

Middle East Studies Association (MESA)
1232 North Cherry Avenue
University of Arizona
Tucson, AZ 85721
602-621-5850

Multimedia Vera International (MVI)
434 South Vermont Avenue
Los Angeles, CA 90020
213-382-2800

Sound Vision
1327 W. Washington Blvd., Suite 105
Chicago, IL 60607
800-432-4262   www.soundvision.com

Southeast Regional Middle East and Islamic Studies Seminar (SERMEISS)
c/o Professor John Parcels
Dept. of English and Philosophy
Georgia Southern University
Statesboro, GA 30460-8023
912-681-5909

Quick Reference Glossary

The study of world religions invariably necessitates the acquisition and mastery of new terminology. The Arabic language is central to the Islamic faith, and consequently most terms related to the religion and its adherents are of Arabic origin. Accurately pronouncing new and unfamiliar words can be intimidating, but with patience and a little help, one can sound almost like a native speaker in no time. This glossary contains the most essential terms for educators teaching about Islam. Some terms will be recognizable, while others may not. Studying this list will give educators a strong foundation for adequatly covering Islam. To facilitate proper articulation, a pronounciation key has been provided in brackets next to the most-preferred spellings of the terms.

A

Abd [ubd] ✳ A prefix used in many Muslim male names in conjunction with a divine attribute of God, meaning "servant." Examples include Abd-Allah ("servant of God"), Abd al-Rahman ("servant of the Most Merciful"), and Abd al-Khaliq ("servant of the Creator").

Abraham ✳ see *Ibrahim*.

Abu Bakr as-Sadiq [a-boo BUCK-er as-SAA-dik] ✳ One of the closest companions of Prophet Muhammad, given the appelation as-Sadiq, "the Truthful." Upon the death of the Prophet in 632 C.E., Abu Bakr became the first Caliph (successor) and served as leader of the Muslim community until his death in 634 C.E.

Adam [AA-dum] ✳ The first human being, created by God as His vicegerent (responsible deputy) on Earth. Muslims believe Adam was the first prophet of God as well, establishing monotheism as the original spiritual system of humankind. Islam does not share with Christianity the doctrine of "Original Sin," instead maintaining that each individual person is born sinless and is responsible for his or her own spiritual state, independent of the actions of other persons, past or present.

Adhan [ad-HAAN] ✳ The Muslim call to worship. The *adhan* consists of specific phrases, recited aloud in Arabic prior to each of the five daily worship times. Upon hearing the *adhan*, Muslims discontinue all activity and assemble at a local *masjid* for formal communal worship.

Ahl al-Kitab [AHL al-kee-TAAB] ✳ Literally, "People of the Book." This term, found in the *Qur'an*, describes adherents of divinely revealed religions that preceded Islam. Most commonly, the term refers to Jews and Christians, and confers upon these two groups a special status within Muslim society, owing to the monotheistic basis of their religions.

Aisha [EYE-ee-sha] ✳ Daughter of Abu Bakr and one of the wives of Prophet Muhammad. Aisha transmitted a large number of the Prophet's *hadith,* which were compiled by scholars in early Islamic history.

Ali ibn Abi Talib [AA-lee ib-un abee TAA-lib] ✳ One of the companions of the Prophet, he was also Muhammad's cousin and son-in-law. He became the fourth Caliph of the early Muslim state in 656 C.E. He is considered the last of the "Rightly-Guided" caliphs by Sunni Muslims, and the first of the *Imams* by Shi'ah Muslims.

Alim [AA-lim] ✻ One who has knowledge. This term refers commonly to a Muslim religious scholar. (pl. *Ulama* [oo-la-ma]).

Allah [al-LAH] ✻ Literally, "The God." Muslims use this Arabic term as the proper name for God. Muslims view *Allah* as the Creator and Sustainer of everything in the universe, Who is transcendent, has no physical form, and has no associates who share in His divinity. In the *Qur'an*, God is described as having at least ninety-nine Divine Names, which describe His attributes.

"Allahu Akbar" [al-LAH-hu UCK-bar] ✻ This phrase, known as the *Takbir*, means "God is Greatest" and is uttered by Muslims at various times. Most often it is pronounced during the daily worship, but Muslims also use it to express happiness, surprise, regret, thankfulness, fear, or approval, thereby reinforcing their belief that all things come from God.

Almsgiving Tax ✻ See *Zakah*.

Angels ✻ See *Mala'ikah*.

(al-) Aqsa [al-UCK-sa] ✻ Name of the holy site located in the city of Jerusalem and referred to in the *Qur'an* as "the farthest *masjid*." The site is believed to be the area from which Prophet Muhammad was miraculously ascended to Heaven in 619 C.E.

Arabic ✻ The language of the *Qur'an*. Arabic is a Semitic language, used throughout the world by Muslims and non-Muslims, Arabs and non-Arabs. Historically, in Muslim civilization Arabic became the language of learning and scholarship, and was the common language for people living as far apart as Spain and China.

"As-Salaam Alaykum" ✻ The traditional, time-honored greeting of Muslims, meaning "Peace be upon you." The appropriate response is *"Wa Alaykum As-Salaam,"* meaning, "And upon you be peace also."

Ayah [EYE-yah] ✻ Literally, "miracle" or "sign." The term is used to designate a verse in the *Qur'an*. There are over 6,600 *ayahs* in the *Qur'an*.

B

Bilal ibn Rabah [bee-LAAL ib-un ra-BAAH] ✻ An early convert to Islam, he was one of the *Sahabah* (companions) of the Prophet. He was also the first *mueddhin* (caller to prayer) in Muslim history.

Bismillah [BIS-mil-LAH] ✻ The Arabic formula pronounced by Muslims at various times for various reasons. The formula *"Bismillah ar-Rahman ar-Raheem,"* means "In the Name of God, the Gracious, the Merciful" and is said before any act or activity of importance, such as travelling, eating a meal, rising from sleep, beginning work, etc.

"Black Muslims" ✻ A term designating African-Americans who adhere to the teachings of the organization known as the Nation of Islam. So-called "Black Muslims" are not to be confused with Muslims (followers of universal Islam) of African-American or African origin. Likewise, the Nation of Islam, a nationalistic organization, is not to be confused with the mainstream, universal world religion Islam.

Buraq [boo-RAAK] ✻ A winged creature, unknown to earth, which transported Prophet Muhammad from Makkah to Jerusalem and thence to Heaven during his miraculous Night Journey and Ascension (*Isra'* and *Mir'aj*) in 619 C.E.

C

Caliph ✻ See *Khalifah*.

Call to Prayer ✻ See *Adhan*.

Charity ✻ See *Sadaqah*.

D

Day of Judgement ✴ Belief in the Day of Judgement is a basic article of faith in Islam. After God ends the present world and order of creation, a day will follow on which He will judge every person according to his or her intentions, deeds, and circumstances. Judgement by God is followed by punishment in Hell or eternal reward in Paradise.

Declaration of Faith ✴ See *Shahadah*.

Deen ✴ A term commonly used to mean "religion," but actually referring to the totality of Muslim beliefs and practices. Thus, Islam as a *deen* is a "complete way of life."

Dhikr [DHIK-er] ✴ Remembrance of Allah [God] through verbal or mental repetition of His divine attributes or various religious formulas, such as "*Soob-han Allah*," meaning "Glory be to God." *Dhikr* is a common practice among all Muslims, but is especially emphasized by Sufis.

Dhimmi [DHIM-mee] ✴ A person belonging to the category of "protected people" (*ahl ad-dhimmah*) within the Islamic state. Historically, Jews and Christians traditionally received this status due to their belief in One God, but others such as Zoroastrians, Buddhists and Hindus were also included. *Dhimmis* had full rights to practice their faith and implement their own religious laws within their communities. In exchange for a guarantee of protection and exemption from military service, *dhimmis* payed a specific tax to the state, just as their fellow Muslim citizens did.

Dome of the Rock ✴ Name of the famous *masjid* in Jerusalem built around 691 C.E. by the Umayyad caliph Abd al-Malik. The rock within the *masjid* structure is believed to be the point from which Muhammad was miraculously ascended to Heaven in 619 C.E.

Du'a [DOO-ah] ✴ Term designating personal prayer, supplication, and communication with God, as distinct from *salah* (formal worship). Muslims make *du'as* for many reasons and at various times, such as after *salah*, before eating a meal, before retiring to sleep, or to commemorate an auspicious occasion such as the birth of a child. Personal *du'as* can be made in any language, whereas *salah* is performed in Arabic.

E

Eid [eed] ✴ *Eid* is an Arabic term meaning "festivity" or "celebration." Muslims celebrate two major religious holidays, known as *Eid al-Fitr* (which takes place after *Ramadan*), and *Eid al-Adha* (which occurs at the time of the *Hajj*). A traditional greeting used by Muslims around the time of *Eid* is "*Eid Mubarak*," meaning "May your holiday be blessed." A special congregational *Eid* worship, visitation of family and friends, new clothing, specially-prepared foods and sweets, and gifts for children characterize these holidays.

Eve ✴ See *Hawwa*.

F

Fard [furd] ✴ A term designating that which is an obligatory (required) belief or practice in Islam. For example, under normal circumstances, performing *wudu* (ritual washing) before offering formal worship is *fard* for Muslims.

Fasting ✴ See *Sawm*.

(al-) Fatihah [al-FAA-ti-HAH] ✴ Arabic name meaning "The Opening," and referring to the opening chapter of the *Qur'an*. This chapter, recited during the daily formal worship, is comprised of seven short verses and summarizes the essential beliefs of Muslims and the obligation of human beings to seek guidance and aid from God alone.

Fatwa [FUT-wa] ✹ A legal ruling in *Shari'ah* (Islamic Law), made by a learned and qualified scholar, usually in response to an unprecedented situation or to address a novel issue.

Fiqh [fik] ✹ Literally "understanding," this term refers to the body of knowledge and legal opinions developed by Muslim jurists and scholars from the primary sources in Islam, the *Qur'an* and the *Sunnah* of Prophet Muhammad. *Fiqh* is essentially the interpretation and application of *Shari'ah* to specific circumstances or issues.

Fitrah [FIT-rah] ✹ An Arabic term designating the innate, original spiritual orientation of every human being towards God the Creator. Muslims believe that God endowed everything in Creation with a tendency towards goodness, piety and God-consciousness, and that one's environment, upbringing, and circumstances serve to enhance or obscure this tendency.

Five Pillars of Islam, The ✹ A term referring to the five core religious practices incumbent upon all Muslims, and which demonstrate a Muslim's commitment to God in word and in deed. They are as follows: *Shahadah* (declaration of faith), *Salah* (formal worship), *Zakah* (mandatory alms-giving tax), *Sawm* (fasting during Ramadan), and *Hajj* (pilgrimage to Makkah).

G

Gabriel ✹ See *Jibreel*.

(al-) Ghayb ✹ Arabic term referring to the unseen world, belief in which is a basic article of faith. Angels, *jinn* and other creations of God inhabit this realm. For Muslims, recognition of al-Ghayb demonstates acknowledgement that human knowledge is limited and that only God is the All-Knowing and All-Powerful.

God ✹ See *Allah*.

H

Hadith [ha-DEETH] ✹ Unlike the verses contained in the *Qur'an*, *Hadith* are the sayings and traditions of Prophet Muhammad himself, and form part of the record of the Prophet's *Sunnah* (way of life and example). The *Hadith* record the words and deeds, explanations, and interpretations of the Prophet concerning all aspects of life. *Hadith* are found in various collections compiled by Muslim scholars in the early centuries of the Muslim civilization. Six such collections are considered most authentic.

Hafiz [HAA-fiz] ✹ One who has memorized the entirety of the *Qur'an*. Thousands of Muslim men and women throughout the world dedicate their time and energy to this tradition, which serves to maintain the *Qur'anic* scripture as it was revealed to Prophet Muhammad over 1,400 years ago.

Hajar [HAA-jer] ✹ One of Abraham's wives who, along with her infant son Isma'il, was settled in Arabia by Abraham. She may be considered the founder of the city of Makkah, since it was a desolate valley prior to her arrival and discovery of the sacred well known as *ZamZam*.

Hajj [huj] ✹ The pilgrimage (journey) to Makkah (in modern-day Saudi Arabia) undertaken by Muslims in commemoration of the Abrahamic roots of Islam. The *Hajj* rites symbolically reenact the trials and sacrifices of Prophet Abraham, his wife Hajar, and their son Isma'il over 4,000 years ago. Muslims must perform the *Hajj* at least once in their lives, provided their health permits and they are financially capable. The *Hajj* is performed annually by over 2,000,000 people during the twelfth month of the Islamic lunar calendar, *Dhul-Hijjah*.

Halal [ha-LAAL] ✹ Arabic term designating that which is deemed lawful in Islam, based on the two authoritative sources, the *Qur'an* and the *Sunnah* of Prophet Muhammad.

Hamzah [HUM-zah] ✳ Uncle of Prophet Muhammad and one of his *Sahabah*. He is fondly remembered by Muslims for his support of the Prophet at a time when most other relatives turned away from him because he called on people to worship God alone.

Haram [ha-RAAM] ✳ Arabic term designating that which is deemed unlawful or forbidden in Islam, based on the two authoritative sources, the *Qur'an* and the *Sunnah* of Prophet Muhammad. Muslims must refrain from all things or actions designated *haram*.

Hawwa ✳ Eve, the wife of Adam. The *Qur'an* indicates that Hawwa was created as an equal mate for Adam, and that both Adam and Hawwa sinned equally when they disobeyed God by eating fruit from the forbidden tree in their garden abode. Upon turning to God in repentence, both were likewise equally forgiven.

Hegira ✳ See *Hijrah*.

Hijab [hee-JAAB] ✳ Commonly, the term *hijab* is used to denote the scarf or other type of head-covering worn by Muslim women throughout the world. However, the broader definition of the term refers to a state of modesty and covering that encompasses a woman's entire body, excluding hands and face.

Hijrah [HIJ-rah] ✳ The migration in 622 C.E. of Prophet Muhammad and members of the Muslim community from the city of Makkah to the city of Yathrib, later renamed Madinah an-Nabi (city of the Prophet) in honor of Muhammad. The Islamic lunar calendar, often called the *Hijri* calendar, is dated from this important event, which marks the beginning of an Islamic state (in Madinah) in which the *Shari'ah* (Islamic Law) was implemented.

Hira [HEE-ra] ✳ The cave on the outskirts of Makkah where Muhammad, at the age of forty, received the first revelations of the *Qur'an*, beginning with the word "Iqra" which means "read." The cave was a favorite place of retreat for Muhammad prior to his call to prophethood, where he could contemplate alone and seek God free from the distractions of the city below.

I

Ibadah [ee-BAA-dah] ✳ Literally, "worship," this term refers to any and all acts which demonstrate obedience and commitment to God. Thus in Islam, visiting the sick, giving charity, hugging one's spouse, or any other good act is considered an act of *ibadah*.

Iblis [ib-LEES] ✳ The personal name of Satan, or the devil, as found in the *Qur'an*. Iblis is believed to be a prominent member of the *jinn*, a class of God's creation. He rebelled against God and was cast out from Heaven. God warns human beings repeatedly in the *Qur'an* that Iblis is an avowed enemy of humankind, whose temptations must be resisted in order to stay on the "Straight Path."

Ibn [ib-un] ✳ Arabic term meaning "son of." Many famous Muslim men in history are known by a shortened version of their names begining with *ibn*. Examples include Ibn Khaldun (a historian), Ibn Sina (a physician), Ibn Rushd (a judge and philosopher), and Ibn Battuta (a world traveler).

Ibrahim [ib-raa-HEEM] ✳ Abraham, a prophet and righteous person revered by Muslims, Jews, and Christians alike as the patriarch (father-figure) of monotheism. Muslims commemorate Abraham's devotion, struggles, and sacrifices during the annual *Hajj* rites.

Ihram [ih-RAAM] ✳ State of consecration into which Muslims enter in order to perform the *Hajj* or *Umrah* (lesser pilgrimage). The term also refers to the specific dress, made of white, unstitched, seamless cloth, donned by pilgrims while in this state. During the *Hajj*, the *ihram* worn by pilgrims serves to reinforce a sense of humility and purity, and human equality in the eyes of God.

Ijma [ij-MAA] ✳ Consensus of opinion among scholars and leaders. *Ijma* is one of the means employed by Muslims for joint decision-making, and for interpreting the *Shari'ah*.

Ijtihad [ij-ti-HAAD] ✷ Term designating the intellectual effort of Muslim scholars to employ reason and analysis of the authoritative sources (*Qur'an* and *Sunnah*) for the purpose of finding legal solutions to new and challenging situations or issues.

Ilm ✷ Arabic term meaning "knowledge." The *Qur'an* and *Hadith* encourage Muslims to constantly strive to increase their knowledge, of both religious and worldly matters.

Imam [ee-MAAM] ✷ Generally, the term *imam* refers to one who leads congregational worship. More broadly, the term also applies to religious leaders within the Muslim community. While *imams* lead worship, give sermons, and perform other duties such as officiating marriages, they are not ordained clergy, nor do they belong to any kind of hierarchy. Also, *imams* do not act as intermediaries between individual worshippers and God. The term Imam has specific authoritative connotations for Shi'ah Muslims.

Iman [ee-MAAN] ✷ Arabic term referring to a state of belief in God and other articles of faith, as well as actual demonstration of belief in practice and behavior.

Injeel [in-JEEL] ✷ Arabic name for the holy scripture revealed to Prophet Jesus. The *Injeel* is roughly analogous to the *Evangelium* of Christianity, and refers to a divine book provided to Jesus by God, as distinct from the Christian Gospels, which are viewed as records of Jesus' life written by his closest contemporaries.

"Iqra" [IK-raa] ✷ Arabic word meaning "to read" or "recite," it was the first word of the *Qur'an* revealed to Muhammad during one of his retreats to the cave of Hira above Makkah. Muslims refer to this word to remind themselves of the importance of acquiring knowledge, "from the cradle to the grave" as Prophet Muhammad said.

Isa [EE-sa] ✷ Jesus, an eminent prophet in Islam. Muslims believe that Mary, the mother of Jesus, was a chaste and pious woman, and that God miraculously created Jesus in her womb. After his birth, he began his mission as a sign to humankind and a prophet of God, calling people to righteousness and worship of God alone. Muslims do not believe Jesus was crucified, but rather that God spared him such a fate and ascended him to Heaven.

Isma'il [iss-ma-EEL] ✷ Ishmael, the elder son of Abraham, born to his wife Hajar. When he was about thirteen years old, Ishmael helped Abraham build the *Ka'bah* as a place for monotheists to worship the One God. He, along with his younger brother Is'haq (Isaac), are considered by Muslims to have been prophets in their own right.

Islam [iss-LAAM] ✷ *Islam* is an Arabic word derived from the three-letter root *s-l-m*. Its meaning encompasses the concepts of peace, greeting, surrender, and commitment, and refers commonly to an individual's surrender and commitment to God the Creator through adherence to the religion by the same name.

Isra' and Mi'raj [iss-RAA, me-RAAJ] ✷ The miraculous "Night Journey" and "Ascension" of Prophet Muhammad, respectively, which took place in 619 C.E. This important event, which took place in the year of Muhammad's wife Khadijah's death, gave strength to him by reaffirming God's support for him. During this event, instructions for the formal Muslim prayer were revealed to Muhammad, making them a cornerstone of Muslim faith and practice.

J

Jahannam [ja-HUN-num] ✷ A term found in the *Qur'an* in reference to Hell, described as a place of torment, sorrow, and remorse. Islam teaches that God does not wish to send anyone to Hell, yet justice demands that righteous people be rewarded and those who insist on evil living without repentance and on denial of God be punished.

Jahiliyyah [JAA-he-LEE-yah] ✳ A term designating a state of ignorance and immorality. This term is commonly used by Muslims to refer to the pre-Islamic era in Arabia, when immorality, oppression, and evil were rampant. Some may use the term to describe aspects of modern living as well.

Janazah [ja-NAA-zah] ✳ The Muslim funeral prayer, performed as a sign of respect and goodwill for a deceased Muslim, immediately prior to burial. The prayer reminds all Muslims of their ultimate mortality, thereby reinforcing an ethic of righteous and God-conscious living.

Jannah [JUN-nah] ✳ A term found in the *Qur'an* in reference to Heaven, described as a place of happiness, contentment, and vitality. A reward for the righteous and God-conscious, Paradise is often described as a blissful garden, where people live in eternal comfort and joy.

Jerusalem ✳ See *(al)-Quds*.

Jesus ✳ See *Isa*.

Jibreel [jib-REEL] ✳ Muslims believe that angels are among God's many creations. Jibreel (Gabriel in English) is believed to be one of the most important angels, as he was reponsible for transmitting God's divine revelations to all of the human prophets, ending with Muhammad. Due to his special role in bridging the divine and human realms, he is referred to in the *Qur'an* as a Spirit (*ruh*) from God.

Jihad [ji-HAAD] ✳ *Jihad* is an Arabic word which derives from the three-letter root *j-h-d*, and means "to exert oneself" or "to strive." Other meanings include endeavor, strain, effort, diligence, struggle. Usually understood in terms of personal betterment, jihad may also mean fighting to defend one's (or another's) life, property, and faith. Because *jihad* is a highly nuanced concept, it should not be understood to mean "holy war," a common misrepresentation.

Jinn ✳ A class of creation in some ways similar to human beings. Though they are non-physical beings, they possess, like humans, a free will. Thus, they may choose to obey or disobey God's commandments, and will ultimately be held accountable for their actions. Occasionally they involve themselves in the lives of human beings, causing confusion and fright, though not all *jinns* are believed to be malevolent.

Jum'ah [JOOM-ah] ✳ The congregational worship performed on Fridays in place of the midday worship. On this special day, Muslims make a extra effort to go to their local *masjid* to listen to the *khutbah* (community address) by the *imam* (worship leader) and to perform the formal worship with their fellow Muslim brothers and sisters.

K

Ka'bah [KAA-bah] ✳ An empty cube-shaped structure located in the city of Makkah (in modern-day Saudi Arabia). Built by Prophet Abraham and his son Prophet Ishmael about 4,000 years ago, the *Ka'bah* stands as the first building dedicated to the worship of the One God. The *Ka'bah* is made of stone, and is covered by a black and gold cloth embroidered with verses from the *Qur'an*.

Khadijah [kha-DEE-jah] ✳ The first wife of Prophet Muhammad, and during her lifetime, the only one. Khadijah was a successful businesswoman in Makkah who employed Muhammad as a merchant/trader because of his well-known reputation for honesty and trustworthiness. The Prophet was married to her for 25 years until her death at the age of 65 in 619 C.E. They had two sons [both died in infancy] and four daughters together.

Khalifah [kha-LEE-fah] ✴ An Arabic term meaning "successor," it refers to the rightful successor of Prophet Muhammad as leader of the *ummah* (worldwide Muslim community). The *Khalifah* (caliph) is not a prophet; rather, he is charged with upholding the rights of all citizens within an Islamic state and ensuring application of the *Shari'ah* (Islamic Law). The immediate successors of Prophet Muhammad, known as the "Rightly-Guided" Caliphs, were Abu Bakr as-Sadiq, Umar ibn al-Khattab, Uthman ibn Affan, and Ali ibn Abi Talib.

Khutbah [KHUT-bah] ✴ The weekly community address given by an *imam* immediately prior to the *Jum'ah* (Friday) midday worship service. The address serves as a venue for leaders to share with members of the congregation religious insights, to discuss Islamic viewpoints on important contemporary issues, and to reinforce teachings of Islam.

Koran ✴ See *Qur'an*.

L

Laylat al-Qadr [LAYL-at al-CUD-er] ✴ Literally, "Night of Power." This term is used in reference to the night in Ramadan, 610 C.E. on which Prophet Muhammad received the first revelations of the *Qur'an*, during his retreat in the cave of Hira above Makkah. Muslims commemorate this night, believed to be the 27th of Ramadan (though unknown for certain), by offering additional prayers and supplications late into the night.

Lunar Calendar ✴ The *hijrah* (migration of Prophet Muhammad from Makkah to Madinah in 622 C.E.), marks the starting point of the Muslim calendar, comprised of twelve lunar months (a lunar year is roughly eleven days shorter than a solar year (365 days), since each lunar month begins when the new moon's crescent becomes visible every 29 or 30 days). Muslims use such a *Hijri* calendar for various religious obligations such as fasting during Ramadan, celebrating the two Eid holidays, and performing the *Hajj*. Many contemporary sources on Islam include both the Gregorian (C.E.-common era or A.D.-*anno domini*) and *Hijri* (A.H.-after *hijrah*) dates for historical events. For example, a citation of 974/1566 corresponds to the date of death of the Ottoman sultan Sulayman "The Magnificent" in A.H. and C.E.(A.D.) values.

M

Madhhab [MADH-hub] ✴ An Arabic term used in reference to a particular "school of thought" in Islam. As Islam spread to new regions outside the Arabian penisula and new social, economic and religious issues arose, many scholars studied the sources of Islam to find permissible and practical solutions that believers could employ to address these issues. Over time, the teachings and thoughts of five respected scholars gained prominence, and Muslims tend to adhere to the "school of thought" of one or another of these scholars. Each school's opinions, while differing to some degree with the others, are considered equally valid as a source of practical guidance for the "lay" Muslim.

Madinah [ma-DEE-nah] ✴ Formerly named Yathrib, Madinah became the center of the first Islamic community and political state after Prophet Muhammad migrated there from Makkah in 622 C.E. The people of Madinah welcomed the persecuted Muslims of Makkah with open arms, establishing a sense of brotherhood and sisterhood viewed as a tangible ideal for Muslims today. Prophet Muhammad died in Madinah in 632 C.E. and was buried in his room adjacent to the city's central *masjid*, which he established.

Makkah [MUCK-ah] ✱ An ancient city where Abraham and Ishmael built the *Ka'bah*. Muhammad, a member of the Quraysh tribe, which traced its lineage back to Abraham, was born in Makkah in 570 C.E. After migrating to Madinah to further the message of Islam, Muhammad returned to Makkah in 629 C.E. with fellow Muslims to reinstitute the age-old monotheistic *Hajj*. In 630 C.E., after the Quraysh violated a peace treaty, Muhammad marched on Makkah and gained control of the city peacefully, thereafter clearing the *Ka'bah* of idols and reintegrating the city into the fold of Islam.

Mala'ikah [ma-LAA-ik-ah] ✱ Angels, a class of God's creations. Angels inhabit the unseen world, and constitute a group of beings who do God's bidding and who perpetually engage in His glorification. Muslims believe each human being is assigned two special angels as recorders — one records a person's good deeds while the other records a person's evil deeds. These records will be summoned on the Day of Judgement and each individual will be called to account for his or her deeds. A few angels are named in the *Qur'an*, such as Jibreel (angel of revelation), Mika'il (protector of holy places), and Israfeel (angel who sounds the horn on Judgement Day, calling all souls to account).

Manarah [ma-NAA-rah] ✱ A tower-like structure, more commonly called a "minaret," from which the *mueddhin* (caller to worship) calls out the *adhan* (call to prayer). The *manarah* is usually located adjacent to the *masjid*, though for architectural reasons they may be placed at various places on the *masjid* grounds for practical as well as decorative effect.

Maryam [MARI-yum] ✱ Mary, the mother of Jesus. Maryam is considered by Muslims to be the most favored of women to God, for her chastity, piety and dedication. Muslims believe she miraculously bore Prophet Jesus in her womb and gave birth to him, while remaining a chaste virgin. The fact that an entire chapter of the *Qur'an* is titled "Maryam" indicates that the lessons of her life are extremely important for Muslims.

Masjid [MUS-jid] ✱ A term meaning "place of prostration," *masjid* designates a building where Muslims congregate for communal worship. The term comes from the same Arabic root as the word *sujud*, designating the important worship position in which Muslims touch their forehead to the ground. Often, the French word *mosque* is used interchangeably with *masjid*, though the latter term is preferred by Muslims. The *masjid* also serves various social, educational, and religious purposes. There are three sacred *masjids* in the world which Muslims hope to visit and pray within: *Masjid al-Haram* in Makkah; *Masjid an-Nabawi* in Madinah; and *Masjid al-Aqsa* in Jerusalem.

Mecca ✱ See *Makkah*.

Medina ✱ See *Madinah*.

Mihrab [mih-RAAB] ✱ A niche in the wall of a *masjid* that indicates the *qiblah*, the direction of Makkah, towards which all Muslims turn during the formal worship. Architecturally, the *mihrab* serves to amplify the voice of the *imam* as he leads the worshippers in prayer.

Minaret ✱ See *Manarah*.

Moslem ✱ See *Muslim*.

Moses ✱ See *Musa*.

Mosque ✱ See *Masjid*.

Mueddhin [moo-ED-dhin] ✱ One who makes the *adhan* [call to worship] from a minaret or other suitable location near a *masjid* prior to the five daily worship times. The *mueddhin* may also perform other duties, such as reciting the *Qur'an* while worshippers assemble at the *masjid* and perform the *wudu* (ritual washing) a few minutes prior to commencement of congregational worship.

Muhammad [moo-HUM-mud] ✸ The prophet and righteous person believed by Muslims to be the final messenger of God, whose predecessors are believed to include the Prophets Adam, Noah, Abraham, Moses, David, Jesus and others. Born in 570 C.E., Muhammad grew up to become a well-respected member of Makkan society. In 610 C.E., he received the first of many revelations that would eventually form the content of the *Qur'an*. Soon after this initial event, he was conferred prophethood and began calling people to righteousness and belief in One God. Muhammad died in 632 C.E., after successfully (re)establishing the religion known as Islam and providing Muslims with a model for ideal human behavior.

Musa [MOO-sa] ✸ Moses, an eminent prophet in Islam. The *Qur'an* contains accounts similar to those in the Hebrew Bible regarding Moses' early life and upbringing. Muslims believe Moses was chosen as a prophet by God, and his mission was to call Pharoah and the Egyptians to believe in One God and cease oppression of the Hebrew peoples. Muslims believe the Torah, a divine scripture, was given to Moses as a guidance for those who heeded his leadership.

Muslim [MOOS-lim] ✸ Literally (and in the broadest sense), the term means "one who submits to God." More commonly, the term describes any person who accepts the creed and the teachings of Islam. The word "Muhammadan" is a pejorative and offensive misnomer, as it violates Muslims' most basic understanding of their creed — Muslims do not worship Muhammad, nor do they view him as the founder of the religion. The word "Moslem" is also incorrect, since it is a corruption of the word "Muslim."

N

Nafs [nufs] ✸ The soul or spirit. Muslims believe that humans are ultimately spiritual beings, housed temporarily in a physical body. The *nafs* represents that core of each individual which exhibits an innate orientation towards God, called *fitrah*, and which passes into a different unknown realm upon a person's physical death in the present world.

"Nation of Islam" ✸ An organization formed in the United States in the 1930s by Elijah Poole (later known as Elijah Muhammad), which gained prominence during the nascent civil-rights movement in the 1950s. In its efforts to uplift and provide self-worth to African-Americans, the nationalist organization espoused a doctrine of black superiority, and posited that God manifested Himself as a human being by the name of W.D. Fard, Elijah Muhammad's instructor. Such doctrines and teachings of the Nation are incompatible with the universal outlook and absolute monotheism of Islam. Unfortunately, much confusion has resulted and continues to exist due to this group's appropriation of certain Arabic terms, values, and ideas from mainstream Islam. Followers of the Nation, often incorrectly called "Black Muslims" number less than 10,000 today. Many thousands of former members entered the fold of universal Islam after the death of Elijah Muhammad in 1975 under the leadership of his son Warith Deen Muhammad.

Night Journey and Ascension ✸ See *Isra' and Mi'raj*.

P

"People of the Book" ✸ See *Ahl al-Kitab*.

Pilgrimage ✸ See *Hajj*.

Prayer ✸ See *Salah* and *Du'a*.

Q

Qari [KAA-ree] ✹ Literally, "a reciter." This term refers to a class of Muslim religious leaders who, due to vocal beauty and skill, publicly recite verses from the *Qur'an*. Such recitations serve to inspire and comfort believers, and are often performed early in the morning or prior to the daily worship services, and also to solemnize important occasions and events.

Qiblah [KIB-lah] ✹ The term used in reference to the direction Muslims face during *salah*, the formal worship. The *qiblah's* focal point is the *Ka'bah*, the house of worship located in the city of Makkah. Depending upon where one is at any given time upon the earth, the *qiblah* direction may vary. From North America, the direction is roughly northeast, and worship halls in local *masjids* are oriented accordingly.

Qiyas [key-YAAS] ✹ Using analogies for the purpose of applying laws derived from the *Qur'an* and *Sunnah* to situations not explicitly covered by these two sources. *Qiyas* is one of the most important tools for interpreting and implementing the *Shari'ah* (Islamic Law).

(al-) Quds [al-KOODS] ✹ Literally, "The Holy," this is the name used by Muslims for Jerusalem. al-Quds is the third holiest city in Islam, following Makkah and Madinah, because of its significance to Islamic history in the broadest sense: the city is important for its role in the time of Prophet Muhammad and in the times of earlier prophets.

Quraysh [kur-AYSH] ✹ One of the major tribes in Arabia, to which Muhammad belonged. When Prophet Muhammad persisted in calling people to worship God alone, most of the Quraysh disavowed him and attempted to thwart his efforts, even going so far as to attempt killing him. Until Prophet Muhammad gained control of Makkah in 630 C.E., the Quraysh continued to plot Muhammad's downfall, after which they acquiesced and entered the fold of Islam.

Qur'an [cur-AAN] ✹ The word *Qur'an* means "the recitation" or "the reading," and refers to the divinely revealed scripture of Islam. It consists of 114 *surahs* (chapters) revealed by God to Muhammad over a period of twenty-three years. The *Qur'an* continues to be recited by Muslims throughout the world in the language of its revelation, Arabic, exactly as it was recited by Prophet Muhammad nearly fourteen hundred years ago. The *Qur'an* is viewed as the authoritative guide for human beings, along with the *Sunnah* of Muhammad. Translations of the *Qur'an* are considered explanations of the meaning of the *Qur'an*, but not the *Qur'an* itself. The spelling "Koran" is phonetically incorrect; the more accurate *Qur'an* should be used.

R

Rak'ah [ruck-AH] ✹ Literally, "a bowing." This term designates one complete cycle of standing, bowing, and prostrating during *salah* (formal worship). Verses from the *Qur'an*, special prayers and phrases are stated in these different positions. Each of the five formal worship times are comprised of varying numbers of such cycles: the morning worship is comprised of 2 *rak'ahs*, the evening worship 3 *rak'ahs*, and the other worship times 4 *rak'ahs*.

Ramadan [ra-ma-DAAN] ✹ The ninth month of the Islamic lunar calendar, *Ramadan* is important because it is the month in which the first verses of the *Qur'an* were revealed to Muhammad. Thus, it is considered a blessed and holy month. Furthermore, *Ramadan* is the month in which Muslims fast daily from dawn to sunset to develop piety and self-restraint.

S

Sadaqah [sa-da-KAH] ✳ Literally, "righteousness." This terms refers to the voluntary giving of alms (charity). *Sadaqah* is distinct from *zakah*, which is a mandatory contribution paid yearly and calculated based on one's wealth or assets. *Sadaqah* can consist of any item of value, and can be provided to any needy person. The *Qur'an* states that God loves those who are charitable and promises great reward and forgiveness for those who give regularly to others in need.

Sahabah [sa-HAA-bah] ✳ A term meaning "companions," commonly used in reference to those followers of Prophet Muhammad who were closest to him in his lifetime, kept frequent company with him, and strove to emulate his sayings and doings. The *Sahabah's* piety, knowledge and love for the Prophet were important factors in the perpetuation of his teachings and the painstakingly careful recording of the his *hadith* in the years following his death.

(as-) Sahih [as-sa-HEEH] ✳ The name applied to two important collections of *hadith*, one (*Sahih Bukhari*) by Muhammad ibn Isma'il al-Bukhari (d. 870 C.E.) and the other (*Sahih Muslim*) by Abu al-Husayn Muslim (d. 873 C.E.). Both collections are considered highly authoritative, due to the collectors' scrupulous methods for verifying the authenticity of the *hadith* contained in them.

Sahur [sa-HOOR] ✳ A light meal taken by Muslims before dawn prior to beginning the daily fast of *Ramadan*. Arising for this meal is an emulation of Prophet Muhammad, since it was his practice to do so, and thus is part of his *Sunnah*.

Salah [sa-LAAH] ✳ *Salah* refers to the prescribed form of worship in Islam, and is one of the "five pillars" of Islam. Muslims perform the *salah* five times throughout each day as a means of maintaining God-consciousness, to thank Him for His blessings and bounty, and to seek His assistance and support in one's daily life.

Sawm [so-um] ✳ *Sawm* refers to the daily fast Muslims undertake during the month of *Ramadan*, and is one of the "five pillars" of Islam. For Muslims, fasting means total abstinence from all food, drink, and marital sexual relations from dawn to sunset. Muslims fast for many reasons, including to build a sense of will-power against temptation, to feel compassion for less fortunate persons, and to reevaluate their lives in spiritual terms.

Shahadah [sha-HAA-duh] ✳ An Arabic word meaning "witnessing," *Shahadah* refers to the declaration of faith ("*La-Ilaha-Illa-Lah Muhammadur-Rasul-Allah*") which all Muslims take as their creed — namely, that there is no deity but God and that Muhammad is the Messenger of God. The *Shahadah* constitutes the first of the "five pillars" of Islam.

Shaykh [shay-kh] ✳ Arabic term meaning "leader" or "chief," often used as a title of respect for learned and respected individuals. In the Sufi tradition, the term has a more specific application, referring to leaders within various *tariqahs* (spiritual orders or groups).

Shari'ah [sha-REE-ah] ✳ Literally "the path," this term refers to guidance from God to be used by Muslims to regulate their societal and personal affairs. The *Shari'ah* is based upon the *Qur'an* and the *Sunnah* of Muhammad, and is interpreted by scholars in deliberating and deciding upon questions and issues of a legal nature.

Shi'ah [SHEE-ah] ✳ Literally, "party" or "partisans," this term designates those Muslims who believe that the rightful successor to Prophet Muhammad should have been Ali ibn Abi Talib, rather than the first caliph Abu Bakr as-Sadiq. Shi'ah Muslims may be found in Iran, Iraq, Afghanistan, Lebanon, Syria, Pakistan, India, and some Gulf States.

Shi'ism [SHEE-ism] ✳ A branch of Islam comprising about 10% of the total Muslim population. In Shi'i Islam, Ali ibn Abi Talib is believed to have been the rightful successor to Prophet Muhammad. Moreover, Shi'ahs believe that Ali was granted a unique spiritual authority, which was passed on to certain of his descendants given the title of *Imam* (leader). The largest group in Shi'ism believes that Ali was the first of twelve Imams, and that the last one continues to exist, albeit miraculously and in a state of occultation (concealment from human view). The teachings of these spiritual leaders are an additional source of *Shari'ah* (Islamic Law), used by Shi'i religious scholars to derive legislation and issue religious opinions.

Shirk ✳ Literally, "association," this term is commonly used to mean association of something other than God with God. For Muslims, God is Absolute, Complete, and Self-Sufficient. To set anything alongside or in place of God as Reality or Divinity is to commit the sin of association. Thus, paganism, or even atheism, are viewed as expressions of *shirk*. According to the *Qur'an*, it is the only sin not forgiven by God, and hence it is critical not to die in the state of *shirk* after having been granted guidance about the Oneness of God (*tawheed*).

Sufi [SOOF-ee] ✳ One who endeavors to achieve direct inward knowledge of God through adherence to various spiritual doctrines and methods. These include repeatedly invoking the Divine Names and reciting other religious expressions, living an austere lifestyle, and participating in various spiritual gatherings usually formed around a spiritual master with the title *shaykh*. Historically, *sufis* have been grouped into organizations known as *tariqahs*.

Sufism [SOOF-ism] ✳ A particular spiritual approach and lifestyle adopted by some Muslims (known as *sufis*), rather than a distinct branch of Islam. Sufism holds that direct and intimate knowledge of God can be achieved through spiritual discipline, exertion, and austerity. Essentially, Sufism is seen as an "inward" path of communion with God, complementing the *Shari'ah*, or "outward" religious law.

Sunnah [SOON-nah] ✳ Literally, this term means habit, practice, customary procedure, action, norm, or usage sanctioned by tradition. More specifically, *Sunnah* refers to Prophet Muhammad's sayings, practices, and habits. The *Hadith* of the Prophet constitute a written record of his *Sunnah*.

Sunni [SOON-nee] ✳ A term designating those Muslims who recognize the first four successors of Prophet Muhammad as the "Rightly-Guided" caliphs, and who attribute no special religious or political function to the descendants of the Prophet's son-in-law Ali ibn Abi Talib. Sunnis hold that any pious, just, and qualified Muslim may be elected Caliph. Sunnis comprise the majority of Muslims, numbering about 90% of the total.

Surah [SOO-rah] ✳ A distinct chapter of the *Qur'an*, designated by a title such as *Abraham*, *The Pilgrimage*, or *The Table-Spread*. An individual verse within a *surah* is called an *ayah*. The *Qur'an* is comprised of 114 *surahs* of varying lengths.

T

Tafsir [tuf-SEER] ✳ Any kind of explanation, but especially a commentary on the *Qur'an*. Translations of the *Qur'an* from Arabic into other languages such as Spanish, Urdu, or English are considered *tafsirs* of the *Qur'an*, since only the original Arabic text actually constitutes the content of the *Qur'an*.

Takbir [tuck-BEER] ✳ See *"Allahu Akbar."*

Talbiyah [tul-BEE-yah] ✳ The name for the set of phrases attributed to Prophet Abraham and uttered by Muslims in emulation of him during the annual *Hajj*. This is the central, ritual recitation of the pilgrimage, recited from the moment pilgrims don the *ihram*, the pilgrim's plain white attire. One of the phrases of the *talbiyah* is "Here I am, Oh Lord, at Thy service. Here I am!"

Taqwa [TUCK-waa] ✳ Condition of piety and God-consciousness that all Muslims aspire to achieve or maintain. It can be said that one's *taqwa* is a measure of one's faith and commitment to God.

Taslim [tus-LEEM] ✳ Name for the greeting of Muslims, "*As-Salaam Alaykum*," meaning "Peace be unto you." The *taslim* is also used at the completion of the ritual worship performed five times daily.

Tawbah [TOW-bah] ✳ Repentence, turning to God to seek forgiveness of sins or other wrong actions. Often a component of the personal prayer known as *du'a*.

Tawhid [tow-HEED] ✳ The doctrine of the "Oneness of God." This is a central tenet of Islam, upon which all other beliefs and doctrines are based. Acknowledging the Unity (Oneness) of God is the primary basis for salvation in Islam.

Torah [tow-RAH] ✳ Arabic name for the holy book revealed to Prophet Moses thousands of years ago. For Muslims, the *Torah* was a scriptural precursor to the *Qur'an*, just as Moses was a predecessor of Muhammad in the history of divinely revealed monotheism.

U

Ulama [oo-la-MAH] ✳ See *alim*.

Umar ibn al-Khattab [OO-mer ib-un al-khut-TAAB] ✳ A close companion of Prophet Muhammad and the second of the four "Rightly-Guided" caliphs. He ruled from 634 to 644 C.E. and developed many institutions, such as a police force and treasury, for the early Muslim state.

Ummah [OOM-mah] ✳ The worldwide community of Muslims, whose population exceeds 1.2 billion. A term used to denote the collective body of believers in Islam.

Umrah [OOM-rah] ✳ The "lesser" pilgrimage to Makkah. This journey to worship at the *Ka'bah* and offer prayers can be performed by Muslims at any time during the year, unlike the *Hajj*, which takes place during a specified period in the twelfth month of the Islamic lunar calendar.

Uthman ibn Affan [ooth-MAAN ib-un af-FAAN] ✳ One of the close companions of Prophet Muhammad, he became the third of the "Rightly-Guided" caliphs. He ruled from 644 to 656 C.E., and is responsible for ensuring the retention of the *Qur'an* in a singular Arabic textual form, which still exists to this day.

V

Veil ✳ See *Hijab*.

W

Walimah [wa-LEE-mah] ✳ A traditional dinner feast provided to wedding guests by the groom's family after a marriage ceremony. Providing a *walimah* was highly recommended by the Prophet, whether it be a grand or humble affair.

Waqf [WUK-uf] ✳ Term designating the giving of material property by will or by gift for pious works or for the public good. Properties with *waqf* status, such as schools or hospitals, remain so perpetually, providing endless benefit to the community and endless Heavenly blessings to the donor.

Wudu [woo-DOO] ✳ The act of ritual purification performed with clean water in preparation for the formal worship, *salah*. *Wudu* serves as an act of physical cleansing as a well as a precursor to the mental and spiritual cleansing necessary when in the "presence" of God. If clean water is unavailable, a ritual purification known as *Tayyamum*, which involves symbolically touching clean earth, may be substituted.

Y

Yathrib [YUTH-rib] ✳ The former name of Madinah, the city in northern Arabia to which Prophet Muhammad migrated from Makkah in 622 CE.

Yawm ad-Deen ✳ Literally "Day of Faith," one of several Arabic terms for Judgement Day. See *Day of Judgement*.

Z

Zabur [za-BOOR] ✳ Arabic name for the holy scripture revealed to Prophet David thousands of years ago. For Muslims, the *Zabur*, analogous to the Christian Psalms, was a scriptural precursor to the *Qur'an*, just as David was a predecessor of Muhammad in the history of divinely revealed monotheism.

Zakah [za-KAAH] ✳ *Zakah* literally means "purification," and refers to an almsgiving tax, roughly 2.5% of one's accumulated wealth, that eligible Muslims pay annually. *Zakah* is one of the "five pillars" of Islam, and is usually collected by local *masjids* or charitable organizations. The funds are distributed to poor and needy persons in the Muslim community. Paying the *zakah* reminds Muslims of the duty to help those less fortunate, and that wealth is a trust from God rather than something to be taken for granted.

www.cie.org

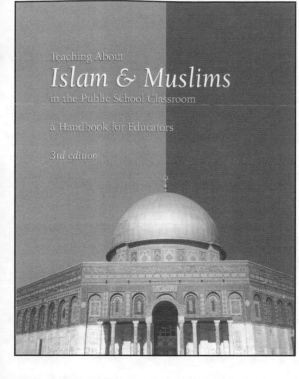

Teaching About Islam and Muslims

in the Public School Classroom

A Handbook for Educators

The third edition of this popular publication helps teachers with the challenging task of teaching about Islam and Muslims. This resource contains:

◆ Information on beliefs and practices of Muslims, including glossary of terms, charts and graphics.

◆ Section on sensitivity regarding Muslim students in public schools and their needs.

◆ Annotated list of recommended books, teaching tools, videotapes and computer resources, grouped by topic.

◆ Other useful information to help teachers meet various state curriculum requirements.

P.O. Box 20186
Fountain Valley, CA 92728
ph. 714-839-2929
fax 714-839-2714
website: www.cie.org
e-mail: info@cie.org

ORDER FORM

Date: _____   E-mail: _____

Name: _____   P.O. No.: _____

Billing Address: _____

City/ST: _____   Zip: _____

Phone: _____   Fax: _____

Shipping Address: _____

City/ST: _____   Zip: _____

Phone: _____   Fax: _____

Qty.	Item	Price Each	Total
	The Emergence of Renaissance *Cross-Cultural Resource Collection*	$75.00	
	Beyond A Thousand and One Night *Literature Sampler*	$50.00	
	Muslim Women Through the Centuries *Teaching Unit*	$15.00	
	The Crusades from European and Muslim Perspectives, *Teaching Unit*	$15.00	
	Images of the Orient: 19th-Century European Travelers to the Muslim Lands, *Teaching Unit*	$15.00	
	Teaching About Islam and Muslims in the Public School Classroom, *Teacher's Handbook*	$11.00	
	Muslim Holidays *Teacher's Guide and Student Resources*	$7.00	
	Strategies and Structures for Presenting World History, *Curriculum Guide*	$15.00	
CA Residents Only: add Sales Tax (7.75%)			
Shipping and Handling (U.S. rates only; inquire about intl. rates): Orders up to $10: $3.00 • $11-$20: $5.00 • over $20: 20% of order			
TOTAL (payment in U.S. Dollars only)			

Please make check, purchase order, or money order in U.S. currency to Council on Islamic Education. Allow 2-3 weeks for delivery.

www.cie.org

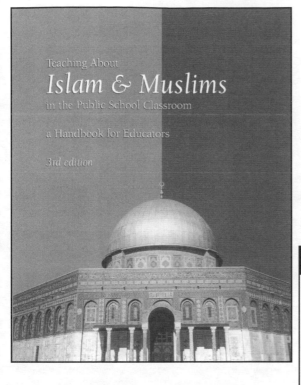